Lake Dis

Mountain Biking

Essential Trails

Design and production by Vertebrate Publishing, Sheffield
www.v-publishing.co.uk

Lake District MountainBiking

Essential Trails

Written by
Chris Gore & Richard Staton

Photography by Andy Heading

Lake District MountainBiking
Essential Trails

Published by Vertebrate Publishing
First published 2006. First reprint 2008.

ISBN 10: 0-9548131-8-9
ISBN 13: 978-0-9548131-8-5

Cover photo: Al Sheldon in Grizedale Forest
All Photography by Andy Heading

Design & production by Nathan Ryder – Vertebrate Graphics Ltd.
Series editor Tom Fenton – Vertebrate Publishing.
www.v-publishing.co.uk

PLEASE GIVE WAY TO HORSES AND PEDESTRIANS.

Contents

ROUTE GRADES
▲ = MEDIUM ▲ = HARD ▲ = EXTREME (see page ix)

KEY TO THE MAP SYMBOLS

Starting point, optional route

Waypoint

Link to another route

Medium ascent, descent

Hard ascent, descent

Very hard ascent, descent

Public house, café

Car park, payphone

Caravan site, caravan & campsite

Campsite, aerial or mast

Dual carriageway
Main road
Wide minor road
Minor road
Residential road
Railway, station, tunnel
Dismantled railway
Track or forest road
Path or old track
Intermittent path
Building, settlement, church
Ruin, sheepfold
Powerline

The representation of a road, track or footpath is no evidence of the existence of a right of way

RIGHTS OF WAY The information on public rights of way is given in good faith, but is not necessarily an accurate record of legal status. Liability is disclaimed for any inaccuracies. Please check with the relevant local authority for the latest amendments.

Public footpath: with path on the ground,
without path on the ground
Public bridleway: with path on the ground
without path on the ground
Permissive path
(permission may be withdrawn)
Long distance path

SCALE: 1 grid square equals 1 kilometre

Lake, jetty, island
Small lake, pond
River, footbridge
Wide stream
Narrow stream
Peat hags
Marshy ground
Farmland
Fell or moorland
Open forest or woodland
Dense plantation
Forest ride or firebreak
Boundary maintained
Boundary remains

On moorland, walls, ruined walls and fences are shown. For farmland, only the outer boundary wall or fence is shown.

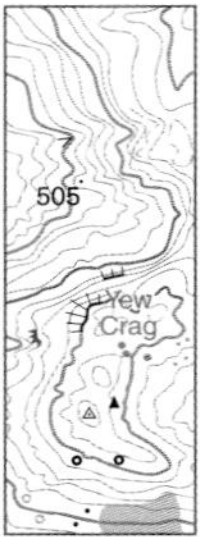

505 Yew Crag

Contour (15m interval)
Index contour (75m interval)
Cave or mine, auxiliary contour
Spot height (in metres – from air survey)
Predominantly rocky ground
Major crag, climbing crag
Spoil heap, sink holes: large, small
O.S. trig pillar, large cairn
Pot hole (some dangerous shafts)
Shaft, large boulder, old workings

Contours change from brown to grey where the ground is predominantly rocky outcrops, small crags and other bare rock.

900m+
825–900m
750–825m
675–750m
600–675m
450–600m
300–450m
150–300m
0–150m

ABBREVIATIONS USED IN ROUTE DIRECTIONS

L = Left » **R** = Right » **RH** = Right-hand

LH = Left-hand » **SH** = Straight ahead

Introduction

When we set out to write this mountain bike guidebook to The Lake District we wanted it to be as far away as possible from those guides that lack information and leave you wondering whether or not the author has actually ridden the route at all; the phrase 'hike-a-bike' jumps to mind! We've been riding the routes included here for over a decade and we have tried to select what we consider to be some of the best routes in the Lakes. There are plenty more out there to be discovered but these are some of the highlights.

When grading the routes we considered the grades used in other areas such as the Seven Stanes; as these are probably the most consistently graded trails in the UK, certainly with regard to how technical you can expect them to be. However, this isn't entirely appropriate for 'The Lakes'. For starters, the terrain wasn't 'built' to be ridden! What our grading tries to do is to take into account, not just the technical nature of the route, but also how much navigation is required and how serious the route is in terms of being in a mountain environment, an aspect that should never be underestimated. For example, we have given 'High Street' a double black; although the route isn't that technical in terms of riding, it is when you consider just how remote the ride becomes and the potential difficulties which could arise from poor navigation. Some of the rides are less serious, taking in the honeypots of Ambleside and, of course, the magnificent Grizedale Forest. We have also tried to show you other areas within the Lakes – places you might not normally consider, but are certainly worthwhile. Rides like Cartmel Fell or the Blawith Loop. There are technical rides for the downhill and singletrack junkies and there are the big days out for the adventurous.

Grizedale Forest deserves a special mention. Grizedale has a lot to offer mountain bikers: man-made trails, bridleways, ancient byways and forest fire roads. In this guide we have covered the forest with a variety of routes which will give the rider a real flavour of what Grizedale has to offer. In doing this, once you know the forest you can start to mix things up a bit to form routes of your own! Beware however; forest riding can be tricky from a navigation point of view so read the descriptions carefully to avoid getting lost, a wrong turn here could have you riding around for hours! It's also worth noting that this is a working forest and so, from time to time, areas of the forest are closed. Please obey all forest signs – they are there for your safety. If in doubt phone the Visitor Centre on **01229 860010**.

Chris Gore and Richard Staton

Acknowledgements

We would like to say thank you to a few people:

Huw Davies, Paul Maine Nick Cotton and Chris's wife Judith for suggesting routes and helping to ride them. Simon Young at Keswick Mountain Bikes for his suggestions for some of the routes, and KMB in general for helping out with broken bikes. Fred Yong, Clair Llyod, Pete Dodd, Steve Heading and Al Sheldon for posing for photos, and Andy Heading for his excellent work in photographing them. Polaris clothing, for their help in supplying kit for photos and Susan Harvey and Harvey Maps for providing their excellent mapping. At Vertebrate Graphics, Nathan Ryder for his design and production work, Jon Barton and Simon Norris for their backing and earlier work, Oliver Jackson for his proof reading and Tom Fenton for his editing and for writing the routes in the north Lakes.

How to Use This Book

Riding in the Lakes

The Lakes are a high and mountainous region, and come with all the dangers common to such regions. Do not rely on this guidebook alone, especially in adverse conditions – take a map and compass and know how to use them.

The trails in the Lakes rank as some of the hardest in the UK. Expect to shoulder your bike in places (possibly even on the descents!) – these are rocky and boggy mountain bridleways, not carefully planned man-made trails. Other than that, think about what we've said about safety on page xii and enjoy some of the best riding in the UK!

The routes

This guide contains the best routes in the Lake District (in our opinion!). The aim is to encourage you to ride new trails in new areas, and to help you get to know the region. Try the routes as suggested, in reverse or joined to neighbouring rides. Once you've ridden a few and got to know what's what, you'll be able to link sections together to create your own rides.

Classics are generally fairly short (although not necessarily easy). Epics are a little longer and climb a little more. Enduros are a step up again, and the Killer Loops are self-explanatory.

Grades

Routes (and notable climbs and descents) are graded blue, red and black, in a similar system to that used at several of the trail centres around the UK.

▲ = Medium ▲ = Hard ▲ = Extreme

The grades are based on average conditions – good weather and not too wet. In a drought routes will feel easier, in the depths of winter, harder. Grades consider technicality, length, climbs, navigation and remoteness – so one 'black' route might be a short all-out techno fest whilst another could be a big endurance challenge with tricky navigation.

As ever, these grades are subjective. How you find a particular route, downhill or climb will be dictated by your own levels of fitness and skill (or bottle).

Maps, Descriptions, Distances

While every effort has been made to ensure accuracy within the maps and descriptions in this guide, things change and we are unable to guarantee that every detail is correct. Please treat stated distances as guidelines.

Please exercise caution if a direction appears at odds with the route on the ground. A comparison between description and map should see you on the right track.

Rights of Way

Countryside access in the UK hasn't been particularly kind to cyclists, although things are improving. We have 'right of way' on bridleways (blue arrows on signs) and byways (red arrows). However, having 'right of way' doesn't actually mean having the right of way, just that we're allowed to ride there – so give way to walkers and horse riders. We're also allowed to ride on green lanes and some unclassified roads, although the only way to determine which are legal and which aren't is to check with the local countryside authority. Obviously, cycle routes are also in.

The very understanding Forestry Commission generally allows cyclists to use its land (again, you'll need to check with them first to be sure). You must, however, obey all signs, especially those warning of forestry operations – a fully loaded logging truck will do more than scuff your frame...

Everything else is out of bounds (unless the landowner says otherwise). Riding illegally can upset walkers, (who have every right to enjoy their day); is, in many cases, technically classed as trespass (meaning you could be prosecuted for any damage caused) and can damage fragile moorland. **Please don't do it**.

Not all tracks are signed, so it's not always obvious whether that great-looking trail you want to follow is an illegal footpath or a legal bridleway. That's why it's a good idea to carry a map with you on every ride.

The Bike

Any half-decent mountain bike will be fine (try and avoid a "£99 special"). A full suspension bike will add comfort and control. A lightweight race number will make hills easier and something with a bit of travel will help on technical descents. We'd pick a compromise somewhere between the three, depending on your personal preferences.

Check everything's working – you won't be going uphill fast if your gears seize but you'll be little quicker than planned if your brakes don't work. Pump the tyres up, check nothing's about to wear through and make sure that everything that should be tight is tight. If you can't do this yourself, visit your local bike shop. The Lakes are always rocky and often boggy, so go big and knobbly, tyre-wise.

Essential Kit

Helmet

"The best helmet is the one that you're wearing". Make sure it fits, you're wearing it correctly and that it won't move in a crash.

Clothing

You need to get your clothing right if you want to stay comfortable on a bike, especially in bad weather. The easiest way to do this is to follow a layering system. Begin with clothing made from 'technical' synthetic or wool fabrics that which will wick the sweat away from your body and then dry quickly, keeping you dry and warm. (Stay away from cotton – it absorbs moisture and holds onto it.) If it's chilly, an insulating layer will keep you warm,

and a wind/waterproof layer on the outside protects from the elements. Layers can then be removed or added to suit the conditions. Padded shorts are more comfortable, but the amount of lycra on display is down to you. Baggy shorts, full length tights and trousers are all available to match the conditions.

Set off a little on the cold side – you'll soon warm up. Don't leave the warm clothes behind though, as the weather can turn quickly.

Gloves

Gloves ward off blisters and numb hands and help keep your fingers warm. They also provide a surprising amount of protection when you come off.

Footwear

Flat pedals/clips-ins – it's your call. Make sure you can walk in them and that they have sufficient tread for you to do so. Consider overshoes if it's chilly.

Other Essentials

As mentioned, take any necessary spares, tools, tube and pump, spare clothes, first aid kit, food and water. Stop short of the kitchen sink, as you'll still want to be able to actually ride your bike.

You'll need something to carry this lot in. We'd suggest a hydration pack, as they allow you to drink on the move and keep excess weight off the bike.

Maps

Harvey Maps:

1:25,000 Superwalker(s) – Lakeland North, Lakeland Central, Lakeland East, Lakeland West, Lakeland South West, Lakeland South East and *Lake District Outdoor Atlas.*

British Mountain Maps:

Lake District Map

Ordnance Survey:

Explorer OL4 The English Lakes: North-western area
Explorer OL5 The English Lakes: North-eastern area
Explorer OL6 The English Lakes: South-western area
Explorer OL7 The English Lakes: South-eastern area

Night Riding

Night riding is ace! It's possible to enjoy an after-work ride in the depths of winter in your favourite off-road playground. But it's a completely different ball game and (hardly surprisingly) there are a few risks to be aware of.

Lights and Batteries

Invest carefully in a lighting system. Consider battery life, weight, number/type of bulbs and power. Fully charge your battery before a ride (sounds like common sense, until you forget). Carry a secondary light source (such as a head torch) for emergencies (it's surprising what you can ride with a commuter light if you have to, although it isn't much fun). Pack a rear light for road sections and keep it clean.

Route Planning and Safety

Choose your ride on the basis of battery life. (Time it yourself, don't necessarily rely on the manufacturer's information.) Allow extra time – you'll be slower in the dark. Stay on ground that you are familiar with at first (night-time navigation in unfamiliar territory demands military expertise) and not too far from home. Ride with a friend. Watch out for the werewolves. Tell someone you're out.

Ride within your limits – trees loom up very quickly in the dark!

General Safety

The ability to read a map, navigate in poor visibility and to understand weather warnings is essential. Don't head out in bad weather, unless you're confident and capable of doing so.

Some of the routes described point you at tough climbs and steep descents that can potentially be very dangerous. Too much exuberance on a rocky descent in the middle of nowhere and you could be in more than a spot of bother, especially if you're alone. Consider your limitations and relative fragility.

Be self-sufficient. Carry food and water, spares, a tube and a pump. Consider a first-aid kit. Even if it's warm, the weather could turn, so take a wind/waterproof. Think about what could happen on an enforced stop. Pack lights if you could finish in the dark.

If you're riding solo, think about the seriousness of an accident – you might be without help for a very long time. Tell someone where you're going, when you'll be back and tell them once you are back. Take a mobile phone if you have one, but don't expect a signal. And **don't** call out the mountain rescue because you've grazed you knee.

Riding in a group is safer (ambitious overtaking manoeuvers excepted) and often more fun, but don't leave slower members riders too far behind and give them a minute for a breather when they've caught up. Allow extra time for a group ride, as you'll inevitably stop and chat. You might need an extra top if you're standing around for a while.

The Lakes can get busy, so ride within your ability, make sure you can slow down fast and give way to other users. Bells might be annoying, but they work. If you can't bring yourself to bolt one on, a polite 'excuse me' should be fine.

On hot, sunny days, slap some Factor 30+ and ALWAYS WEAR YOUR HELMET!

Mountain Rescue

In the event of an accident requiring mountain rescue assistance:
Dial 999 and ask for POLICE – MOUNTAIN RESCUE.

Rules of the (Off) Road

1. Always ride on legal trails.
2. Ride considerately – give way to horses and pedestrians.
3. Don't spook animals.
4. Ride in control – you don't know who's around the next corner.
5. Leave gates as you find them – if you're unsure, shut them.
6. Keep the noise down and don't swear loudly when you fall off in front of walkers.
7. Leave no trace – take home everything you took out.
8. Keep water sources clean – don't take toilet stops near streams.
9. Enjoy the countryside and respect its life and work.

Planning Your Ride

1. Consider the ability/experience of each rider in your group.
   Check the weather forecast. How much time do you have available?
   Now choose your route.
2. Study the route description before setting off, and cross-reference it with the relevant map.
3. Bear in mind everything we've suggested about safety, clothing, spares and food and drink.
4. Get out there and get dirty.

Thanks to:

mountain bike rides

SECTION 1 – CLASSICS

SECTION 2 – EPICS

SECTION 3 – ENDUROS

SECTION 3 – KILLERS

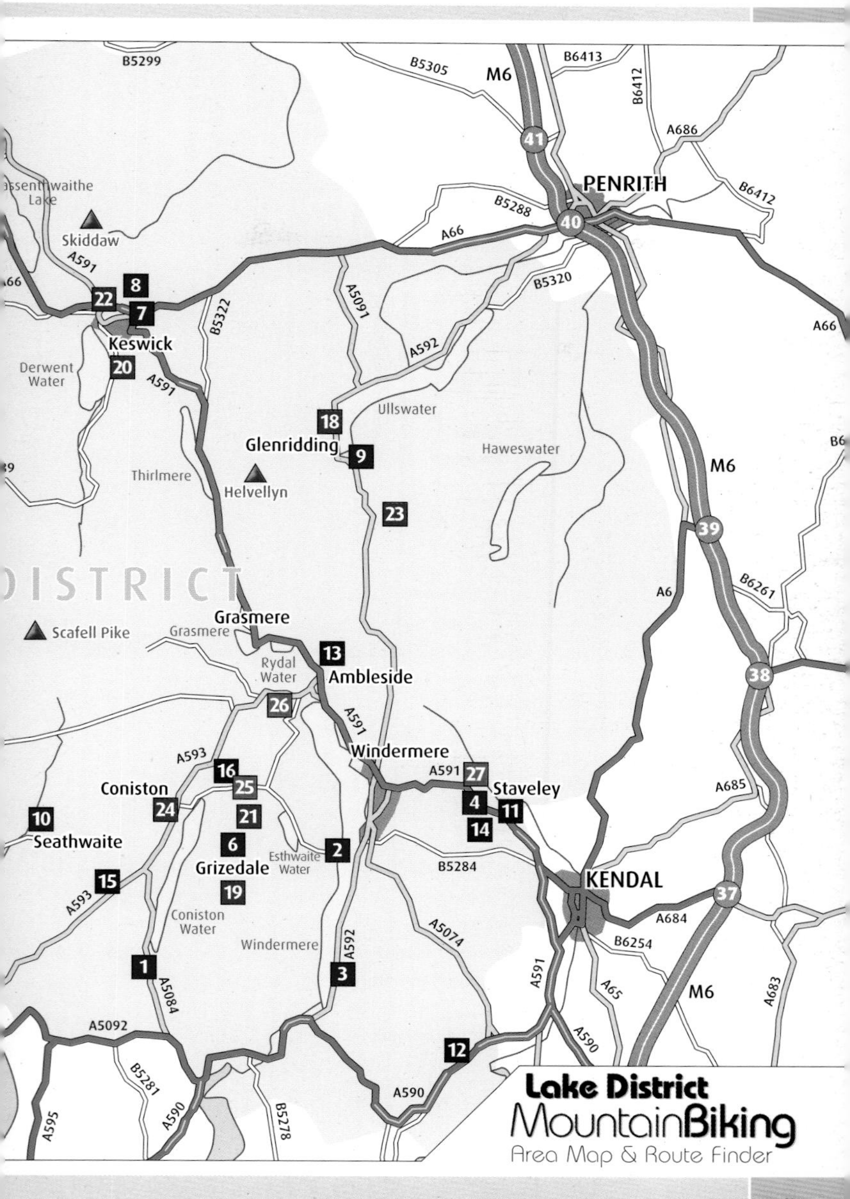
Lake District
MountainBiking
Area Map & Route Finder
PENRITH
KENDAL
Keswick
Glenridding
Grasmere
Ambleside
Windermere
Staveley
Coniston
Seathwaite
Grizedale
Skiddaw
Helvellyn
Scafell Pike
Derwent Water
Thirlmere
Ullswater
Haweswater
Grasmere
Rydal Water
Esthwaite Water
Coniston Water
Windermere
DISTRICT
M6
A66
A591
A592
A593
A5084
A5092
A590
A595
A5074
A5091
A684
A685
A65
A683
A686
A6
B5299
B5305
B6413
B6412
B5288
B5320
B5322
B6261
B5284
B6254
B5281
B5278
41
40
39
38
37
1
2
3
4
6
7
8
9
10
11
12
13
14
15
16
18
19
20
21
22
23
24
25
26
27

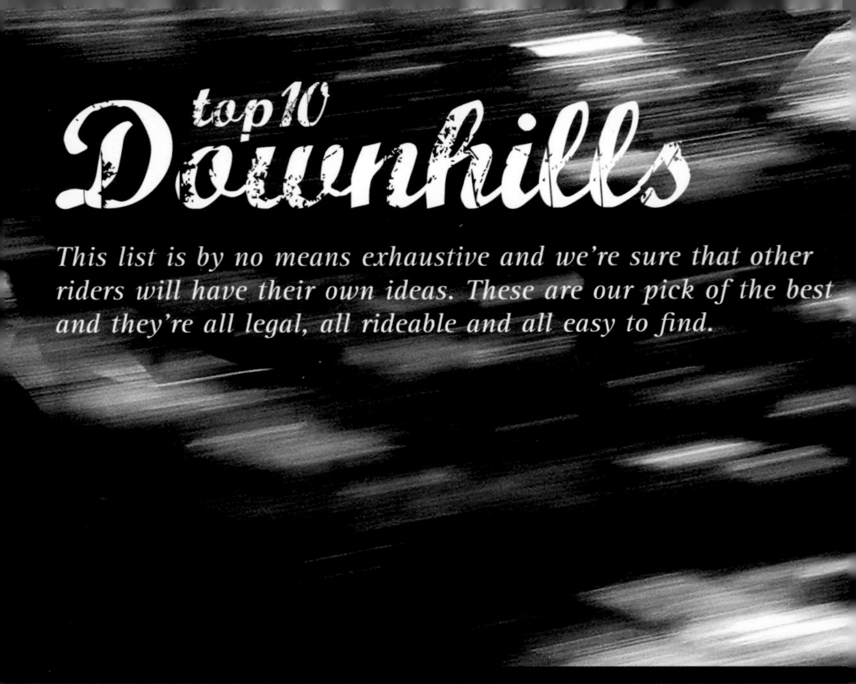

top10 Downhills

This list is by no means exhaustive and we're sure that other riders will have their own ideas. These are our pick of the best and they're all legal, all rideable and all easy to find.

1

Garburn Pass to Kentmere (Garburn Pass) GR NY 435 044 – 454 044

Monster descent some good man laid obstacles; steep with great hairpins.

2

Parkamoor to High Nibthwaite (Parkamoor & Tilberthwaite) GR SD 306 924 – 294 898

Long descent on a good track; not too technical but fast.

3

'The Fox' – Esthwaite (Grizedale & Esthwaite) GR SD 345 952 – 357 955

Starts of with undulating terrain, then really kicks off with some varying technical section.

4

Breasty Haw to Minor Road (Grizedale Forest) GR SD 344 929 – 354 937

Downhill with singletrack, drop offs and steep off-camber corners. Gets steeper towards the end.

5

Lawson Park to Low Bank Ground (Grizedale) GR SD 322 950 – 317 968

If it weren't for the gate this would be one of the best downhills anywhere, nothing technical, just fast.

Walna Scar to Coniston **(Walna Scar)** GR SD 258 964 – 301 974

Stupendous, some good steep hairpins and technical rock steps; lower your saddle and enjoy.

Whiteside End to Kentmere Hall Farm **(Garburn Pass)** GR NY 447 029 – 451 042

Just let the brakes off and go. Mind the right-hander at the end!

Natty Bridge to Stephenson Ground **(Seathwaite & Dunnerdale)** GR SD 242 946 – 235 932

Starts just above Natty Bridge where the footpath and bridleway split. Exposed start, superb singletrack downhill thereafter.

The River Bed **(Grizedale & Esthwaite)** GR SD 326 952 – 330 943

Brilliant, just how brave are you? Let go of the brakes and be rewarded.

Watendlath to Rosthwaite **(Borrowdale)** GR NY 270 160 – 259 150

Steep and rocky. Make that very steep and very rocky!

SECTION

Classics

A quick blast after work, a night loop you can finish before your lights die, or a ride to squeeze in when you're short of time. That's a classic. Relatively low on distance and never taking you too far from the start, these are still good, solid rides. Short but not necessarily easy.

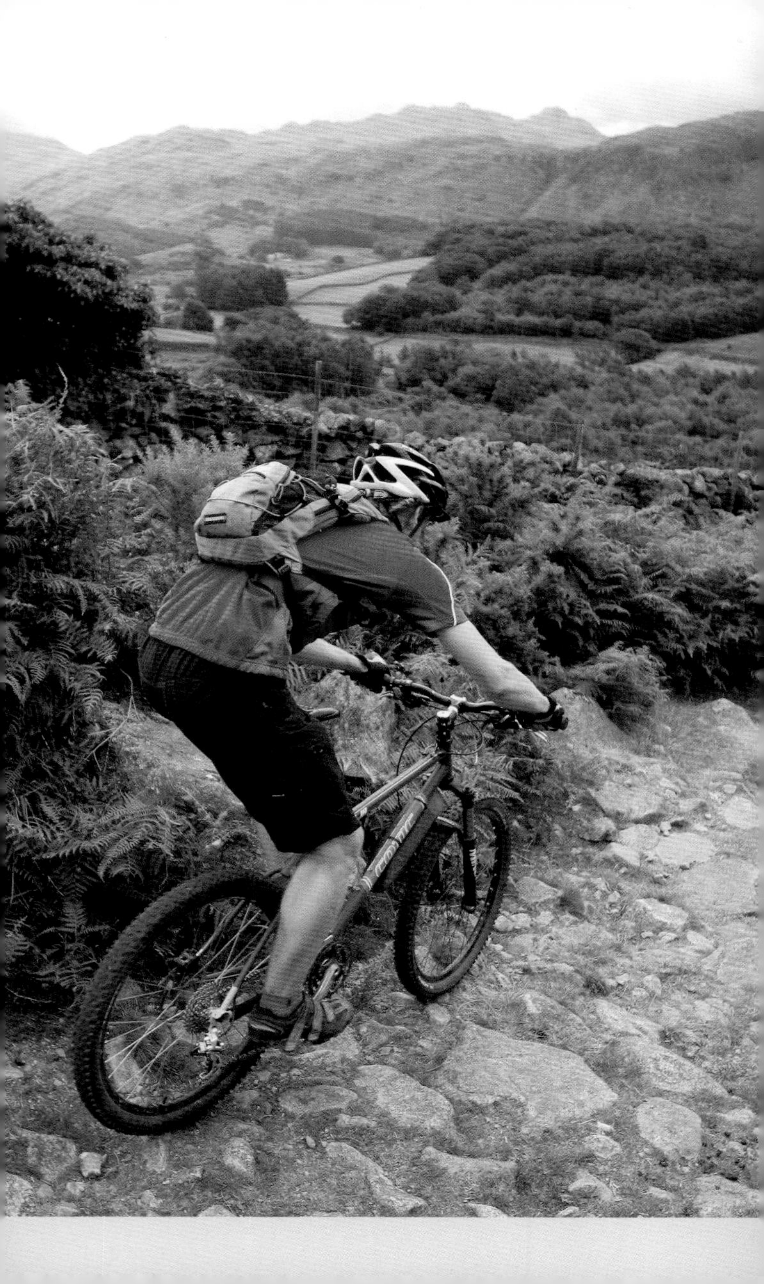

Classics
route finder

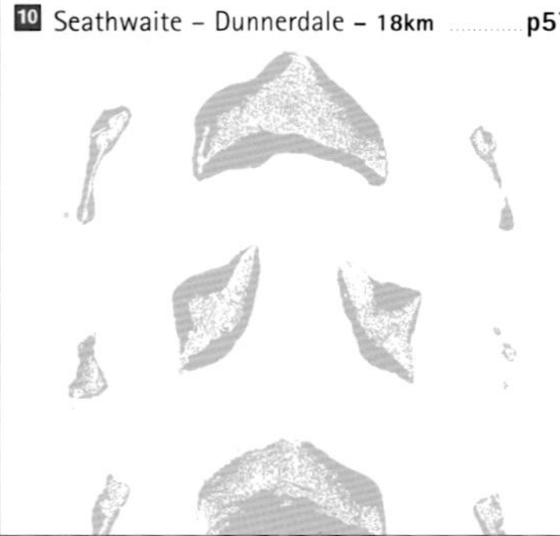

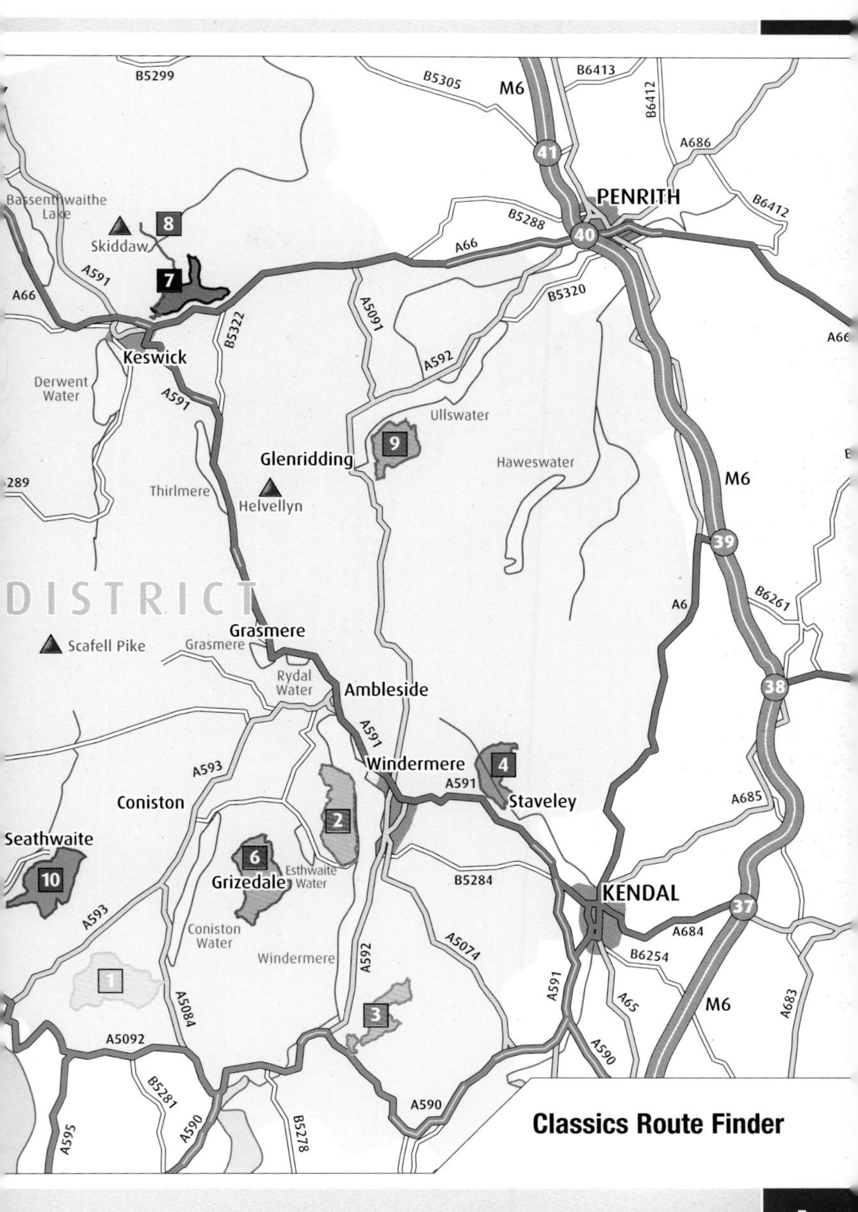

Classics Route Finder

BLAWITH SINGLETRACK

Blawith Loop

12km

Introduction

A great ride for those looking for some decent mountain biking but wanting to avoid the rigours of anything too technical. It is also a good ride for avoiding the hotspots of the Lake District – it really does feel remote on Woodland Fell and Subberthwaite Common.

The Ride

This route takes an anticlockwise course from Blawith on quiet lanes, farm tracks and some great singletrack. The views on Woodland Fell are fantastic, as is the descent off the fell. At Spunham, the ride takes you along tracks and quiet lanes with a stiff climb before another bridleway takes you over Subberthwaite Common. After Birchbank Farm the trails become a little vague, but continue eastwards to Kiln Bank and Raisthwaite Lane before heading back to Blawith.

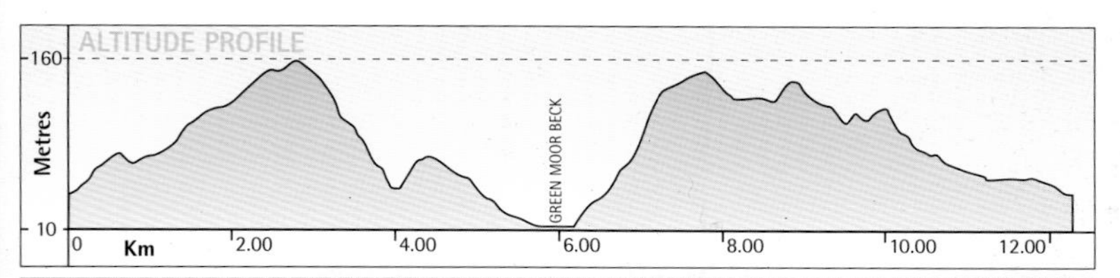

BLAWITH LOOP **GRADE: ▲**

DISTANCE: 12KM

TOTAL ASCENT: 368M

START/FINISH: BLAWITH CHURCH

GRID REFERENCE: SD 288 883

PARKING: IN FRONT OF BLAWITH CHURCH

CAFÉ: BLUEBIRD CAFÉ, CONISTON Tel: 01539 441 649

PUBLIC HOUSE: RED LION, LOWICK BRIDGE Tel: 01229 885 366

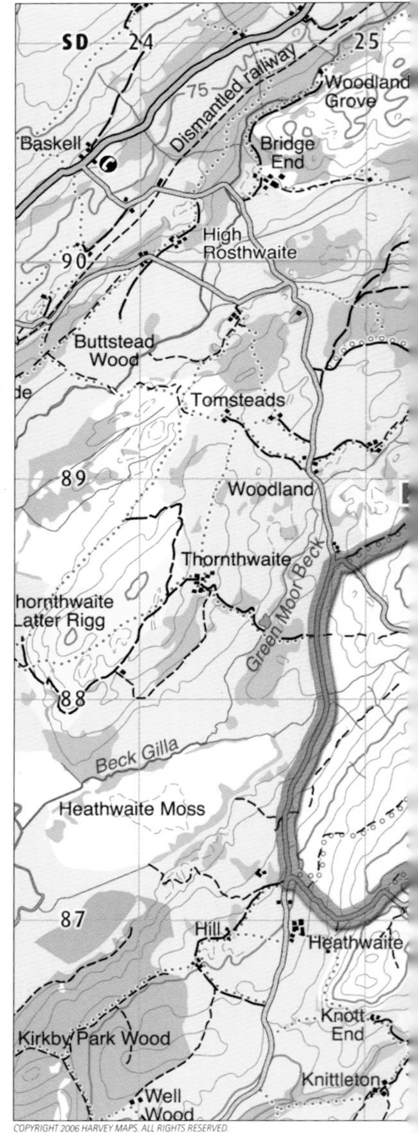
SD
24
25
Dismantled railway
75
Woodland Grove
Baskell
Bridge End
High Rosthwaite
90
Buttstead Wood
Tomsteads
89
Woodland
Thornthwaite
Green Moor Beck
hornthwaite Latter Rigg
88
Beck Gilla
Heathwaite Moss
87
Hill
Heathwaite
Knott End
Kirkby Park Wood
Knittleton
Well Wood

Yew Bank
26
27
28
29
211
Blawith Fells
Beacon Fell
225
Strands Beck
150
Beacon Tarn
Climb Stile
Coulter Stone
Lake Bank
High Nibthwaite
221
Allan Tarn
Mere Sike
Water Yeat
Cockenskell
Greenholme Be
p125 Grizedale & Parkamoor Loop
2
Appletree Holme
150
Blawith Knott
225
247
Blawith
Tottlebank
A5084
Great Knott
Ivy Tree
Lin Crag Farm
Birch Bank
4
Kiln Bank
Crooked Birch
Heads Wood
Subberwaite Common
Lowick Bridge
Bay Bottom
Gawthwaite Land
135
225
Blawith Loop

Directions – Blawith Loop

S From the church in Blawith, take the lane opposite, heading west, bearing **R** at the fork. At the next fork after a cattle grid bear **R** again (the left fork is signed *Tottlebank Only*). After 800m the road reaches a T-junction.

2 Turn **R** then immediately **L** on to a bridleway signed *Woodland & Cumbria Way*. Follow the bridleway – superb riding – **ignoring** turnings until you reach the highest point of Woodland Fell amidst stunning scenery. At the bridleway fork soon afterwards, bear **R** and head downhill. A great descent takes you to Green Moor. **Don't** cross the river, but keep **L** heading south and uphill. The track levels off and then descends to join a farm track at Spunham.

3 Turn **L** along this track, **ignoring** all turnings, to join a metalled road. Turn **R** and then **L** at the junction, signed *Grizebeck*. Follow this road south for 3.7km to a 3-way junction. Turn sharp **L**, (**ignore** the bridleway signed *Tottlebank* on the left), climbing steeply up the hardest climb on the route. Turn **L** onto a bridleway at a sharp right-hand bend shortly before the road begins to descend. The bridleway runs east past a small tarn, becoming a little vague – don't worry, just keep heading east.

4 At the road, go **SA** down the lane opposite, almost immediately turning **L** onto a lane leading to Birch Bank Farm. Turn **L** onto a bridleway just in front of the farm and turn **R** through the first gate reached after a small rise (the track ahead goes on to Tottlebank). Quickly pass through two more gates and follow the vague bridleway, keeping the wall to your right and heading west. At Mill Moss, go through another gate and join a better trail. Follow this to the buildings at Kiln Bank, dismount and walk **SA** through the farmyard (signed *Cumbria Way*) onto the tarmac of Long Lane. Descend to a T-junction and turn **L** back to Blawith.

Making a day of it

Head west from Blawith and you'll quickly pick up the **Grizedale – Parkamoor** route *(page 125)* which will lead you into the wonderful Grizedale Forest.

NEAR BASECAMP

Claife Heights

15km

Introduction

A ride around Claife Heights really is an ideal introduction to Lakes riding: a ferry ride on Lake Windermere, a trolley along the scenic shores of the Lake and then steady riding on wide tracks with some good climbs and superb downs, (not too scary), on open land. We have also given you a choice of finishes: either stop at the Sawrey Hotel for a pint and a short ride back to the ferry on the road, or take the more technical return route over Claife and onto a great downhill (a bit more technical). This route would make a great evening ride, or a nice family outing with picnic potential at Moss Eccles Tarn.

The Ride

Starting from the ferry, the ride follows the picturesque west shore of Windermere, passing Belle Isle and various moored yachts (depending on time of year) and up to Belle Grange. The route then heads inland to High Wray and takes forestry tracks past Basecamp outdoor centre. Steady climbing on generally good tracks leads to Claife, with each uphill followed by a good descent. The run down from Claife is one of these: a fantastic rolling downhills through open land that carries you past various tarns eventually to bring you out at the Sawrey Hotel. From here, head back to the ferry, either directly along the road or, a better option, over to Harrow Slack, via an uphill start and a great technical descent.

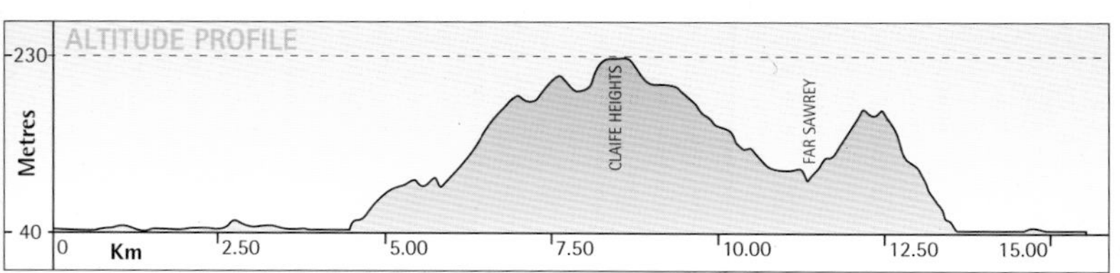

CLAIFE HEIGHTS **GRADE: ▲**

DISTANCE: 15KM
TOTAL ASCENT: 512M
START/FINISH: FERRY PORT ON WEST SIDE OF WINDERMERE
GRID REFERENCE: SD 388 955
PARKING: AT FERRY (EXPENSIVE) OR ON THE WEST SHORE OF WINDERMERE (SD 387 974)
PUBLIC HOUSE: SAWREY HOTEL (OR NUMEROUS IN BOWNESS)
CAFÉ: BOWNESS

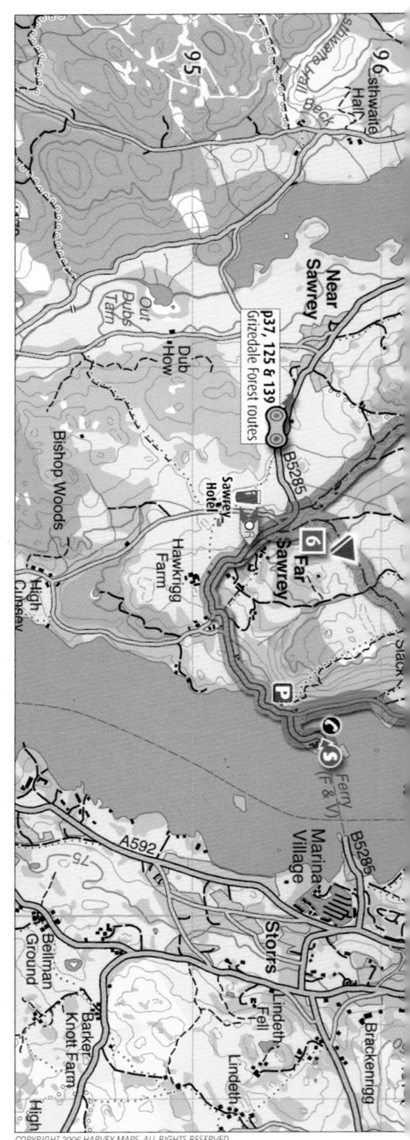
Near Sawrey
p37, 125 & 139
Grizedale Forest routes
B5285
Out Dubs Tarn
Dub How
Bishop Woods
Sawrey Hotel
Hawkrigg Farm
6
Far Sawrey
High Cunsey
Ferry (F & V)
Marina Village
A592
Storrs
Bellman Ground
Barker Knott Farm
Lindeth Fell
Lindeth
Brackenrigg
High

Claife Heights

Directions – Claife Heights

S From the ferry go **SA** on a metalled road, turning **R** at the road junction on a left-hand bend by the lake, heading along the west shore of Windermere. After the second cattle grid, the road turns to track. Follow this, (great undulating riding) for 2km to Belle Grange. Go **SA**, ignoring the bridleway on the left, following bridleway signs to High Wray.

2 At the metalled road by the car park, follow the road uphill, **ignoring** the bridleway on the right. The road goes through the farm at Beyond Fields to a junction. Turn **L**, then, after 20m, turn **L** again onto a dirt track signed *Basecamp*, with a bridleway signed *Claife Heights*.

3 The track continues uphill. At the fork, bear **R** and go through a gate with many padlocks, following the bridleway signed *Guide Posts*. As you crest a rise and start to descend, bear **R** at the fork. Go **SA** at the crossroads onto a bridleway signed *Ferry/Far Sawrey*.

4 Turn **R** at the next crossroads onto a bridleway signed *The Sawreys*. This is not obvious – the track ahead looks good but is only a footpath, while the track you need looks narrow, steep and uninviting. For the strong, it is a harsh ride, while for others it is a short push. At the junction with a wider trail, turn **R** and follow the track to a gate. Go through the gate and enjoy the undulating but mainly downhill ride past the tarns and livestock.

5 At the fork, bear **L** through the gate signed *Far Sawrey*. Turn **R** at the metalled road and then **L** at the junction with the main road. OR Stop off at the Sawrey Hotel for a quick drink and a bite to eat, and then take the quick route back to the ferry by following the main road all the way to the lake.

6 Turn **L** onto the bridleway by the phone box and follow the trail uphill. After the first gate, bear **R** at the fork, still heading uphill. At the next gate, go **SA**, still on the bridleway. After one more gate, start a fun and technical downhill, which leads back down to your outward route along the shore of Lake Windermere. Turn **R** and retrace your steps to the ferry.

Making a day of it

A short distance on the road will take you to Grizedale Forest. Try the **Grizedale Loop** on *page 37*, the purpose-built singletrack or one of the family trails there.

ON CLAIFE HEIGHTS

GREEN LAKES SCENERY

Cartmel Fell

18km

Introduction

This is a hidden gem of a ride, taking in the tracks and trails around the Cartmel Fell area and the forest of Chapel House Plantation. This area is seldom visited by the hordes of bikers and walkers found in the main areas of the Lakes and is a pleasure to ride. The road riding does little to detract from this route as it is on quiet roads and lanes. This is not a technically hard ride, so would suit those aspiring to improve their bike skills, especially if the extra loop to Staveley in Cartmel is taken.

The Ride

From the car park, a steep bit of tarmac soon plateaus, then it's downhill with some sharp bends to Strawberry Bank. A quiet road heads off to Cartmel Fell but a bridleway is taken before this is reached. A generally good bridleway is followed over fells and through woods to the picturesque Sow How Tarn. A little further on and the ride joins Sow How Lane. A short blast downhill through Foxfield ensues before fantastic undulating terrain to Simpson Ground. From here the ride leads to Chapel House Plantation, with some good singletrack leading onto forestry roads. There is a choice of finishes: either follow the forestry roads back to Sow How lane and Gummer's How or some downhill singletrack taking you to Staveley in Cartmel, then back up the forestry roads to join the other finish.

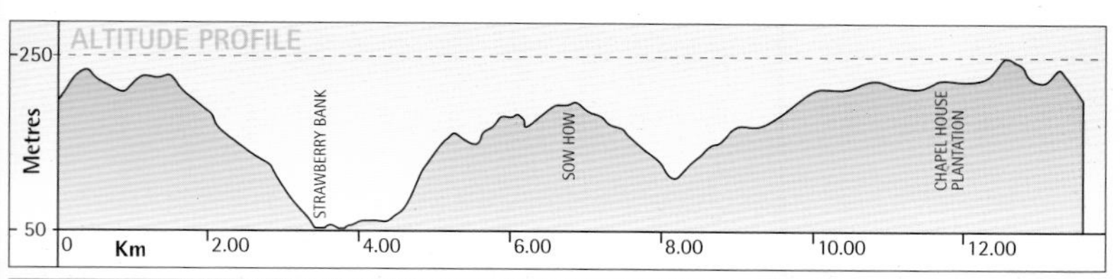

CARTMEL FELL **GRADE: ▲**

DISTANCE: 18KM

TOTAL ASCENT: 700M

START/FINISH: GUMMER'S HOW CAR PARK

GRID REFERENCE: SD 389 876

PARKING: GUMMER'S HOW CAR PARK

CAFÉ: FELL FOOT PARK

PUBLIC HOUSE: MASONS ARMS, CARTMEL FELL Tel: 01539 568 486

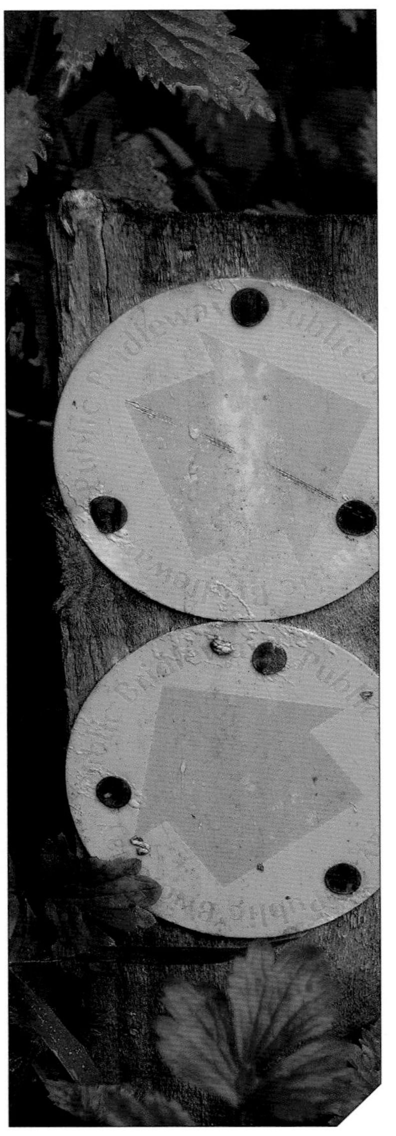

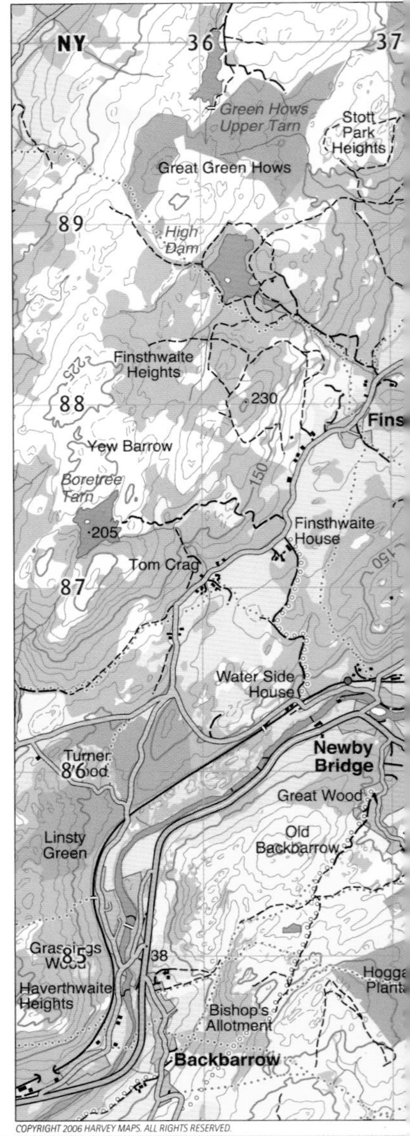
NY
36
37
Green Hows Upper Tarn
Stott Park Heights
Great Green Hows
89
High Dam
Finsthwaite Heights
225
88
230
Yew Barrow
Boretree Tarn
150
205
Finsthwaite House
Tom Crag
87
Water Side House
Newby Bridge
Turner Wood
86
Great Wood
Linsty Green
Old Backbarrow
Grassings Wood
85
38
Haverthwaite Heights
Bishop's Allotment
Backbarrow

Cartmel Fell
Gummer's How
Staveley-in-Cartmel
Mason's Arms
Astley's Plantation
Simpson Ground Reservoir
Chapel House Plantation
High Loft Wood
Low Loft Wood
Sow How
Raven's Barrow
Foxfield
Gateside
The Ashes
Lightwood
Whinny Knott
Birch Fell Plantation
Blake Holme Plantation
Bare Allotment
Ludderburn Park
Addyfield
Haycote Farm
Goswick Hall
Strawberry Bank
Burblethwaite Hall
Heights Tarn
Duck Tarn
Sow How Tarn
Spannel Beck
Town Head
Blake Holme
Chapel House Wood
Chapel House
Raven Scar
Barrow Banks
Bog End Moss
Simpson Ground
Pattison How
Gill Wood
Crag Wood
Mill Wood
Thorphinsty Hall
Cow Head Wood
High Tarn Green
Owlet Lands Wood
Low Tarn Green
Hare Hill
Barrow Wife Hill
Barrow Wife
White Stone
Height
Fiddler Hall
Fair Rigg
Byre Bank

Directions – Cartmel Fell

S Turn **R** out of the car park a grind uphill for a short distance. This tends to hurt the lungs and legs if you don't warm up, but it is soon over. **Ignore** all turnings until you reach a very fast downhill, topped off with some very tight bends near Strawberry Bank – be careful!

2 Go past the Mason's Arm (or stop if you feel the need) and, just after a left-hand bend, turn **R** signed *High Newton, Cartmel Fell.* Follow this pleasant lane downhill. Pass a phone box and a footpath signed *Pool Garth* on the left and climb steeply round a right-hand bend. Just after this, turn **R** through a gate (there are two other gates on the opposite side of the lane).

3 After a short steep stretch, the track splits. Fork **L** through a gate onto a bridleway signed *Sow How.* After the gate the track appears to split again – follow the **R** fork.

4 Follow the grassy bridleway to an unmarked T-junction and turn **R**. Pass through a gated wall and continue **SA**, passing to the **R** of Heights Cottage. Follow the bridleway back **L** (signed) following the wall, and go through a gate into the woods, then through another gate and out of the woods. The very picturesque Sow How tarn is in front of you, unfortunately this is privately owned, so carry on and bear **L** in front of the Tarn (signed), which then brings you to a T-junction with Sow How Lane.

5 Turn **L** and go through a gate, to Foxfield and a metalled lane. **Ignore** turnings and stick to the road. After a downhill in the woods go through a gate, and after 150m, turn **R** onto a track, crossing under the electricity lines.

6 After a short distance, go through two gates, a great undulating track leads to Simpson Ground. Turn **R** at the T-junction – bridleway signed *Staveley in Cartmel*, go through the gate and into the woods, this is Chapel House Plantation.

7 Turn **L** onto the first wide trail going uphill – if you arrive at the reservoir, you've missed it! A great piece of singletrack runs through the woods and ends at the forestry road.

Optional Route

Turn **L** along the forestry road and, after a short distance, turn **R** on a left-hand bend onto a signed bridleway. A steep, bouldery and technical trail ends at a fire road. Go **SA** over this and through a deer gate to follow singletrack through the scrub. After the next deer gate, the track crosses open fell and descends through the woods to Staveley in Cartmel.

At the road by the phone box, turn **L** and follow the road to Chapel House Wood car park. Turn **L** uphill onto the forestry road, pass the bridleway crossroads that you previously came down and continue to a sharp right-hand bend. Go **SA** to rejoin the main route.

8 Turn **R** on the forest road. On a sharp left-hand bend, turn **R**, bearing **L** where the track forks a little further on (to the right is a marked footpath). An overgrown forestry track gives some good riding.

Note: *this is a forestry road and can be out of commission at anytime due to work being carried out within the forest.*

9 At the T-junction, turn **L** and follow the track to a double gate. Go through this and onto the road – this is Sow How Lane. Turn **L** and ride to a T-junction. Turn **L** again and back to the car park.

Making a day of it

There are some pleasant bridleways to the north of this ride, towards Bowness. Follow the road north from Strawberry Bank to find them.

Garburn Pass

15km

Introduction

A great little route, crossing one of the classic Lakeland passes. Off-road for the vast majority of its length, the route features some seriously technical climbing (and descending, if you take the option of reversing it) and some fast, fun descents. A route for experienced riders, crossing high mountain country. The main feature of the route is most definitely the climb up the Garburn Road from Kentmere. You might clean it, you might stop and play around until you conquer individual sections, or you may very well end up shouldering your bike. Believe me, it's worth it in the end! Reversing the route gives an easier climb and a more technical descent.

The Ride

Starting from Ings, the route climbs the hill over to Kentmere. A brief section of tarmac, a couple of tricky sections of climbing, some wide lines and a little rolling singletrack lead to the fast descent to Kentmere Hall. The route then heads out of the valley up one of the Lake's most famous old roads, Garburn Pass. It's rocky, it's steep and it's long. If you can clean this then you're doing well! The climb is soon rewarded with a fantastic decent down into Troutbeck. Try to stay onboard as you attempt to look at the magnificent view and look where you're going at the same time! Either reverse the route (recommended) or drop easily on tarmac to Ings.

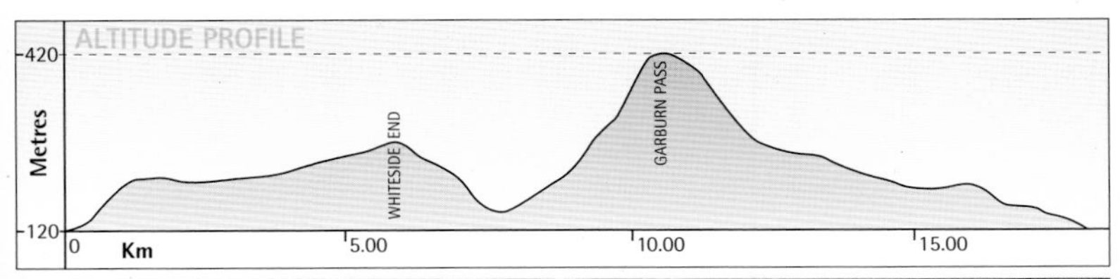

GARBURN PASS **GRADE: ▲**

DISTANCE: 15KM
TOTAL ASCENT: 476M
START/FINISH: WATER MILL PUB IN INGS
GRID REFERENCE: 444 987
PARKING: ON THE ROAD NEAR THE PUB, PLEASE PARK RESPONSIBLY
CAFÉ: KENTMERE IN SUMMER OR WILF'S Tel: 01539 822 329
PUBLIC HOUSE: WATERMILL INN, INGS Tel: 01539 821 309

Heathwaite
High Lickbarrow
School Knott
Grandsire
Mill Beck
Bannerrigg Farm
Grove
Banner Rigg
Orrest Head
Common Wood
The Common
The Causeway Farm
Near Orrest
Far Orrest
Allen Knott
Low Longmire
High Hay Wood
Bishop Plantation
Borrans Reservoir
High Borrans
High House
Heaning
Blackmoss
Yews
High Fairbank
Gowan Bank Farm
Fairbank Farm
Brownspring Coppice
Lily Fell
New Hall
A591
Hill Farm
Grassgarth
Hugill Hall
Low House
Raw Ghyll
High Reston Farm
Reston Scar
Black Crag
River Gowan
The Heights
Hugill Fell
Fellfoot
Goose Howe
Browfoot
Ulthwaite Bridge
Croft Head
Pool Scar
Millrigg Knott

Garburn Pass

Directions – Garburn Pass

S From the Water Mill (the Ambleside/eastern) end of Ings, cross the A591 and head up Grassgarth Lane. Climb the lane for 600m to a bridleway on the **R**, with the caravan site visible down to your left. Follow the bridleway, climbing easily at first, but then with more difficulty near the top, to a gate.

2 Pass through the gate and follow the walled track to the **L**, continuing uphill. The bridleway soon reaches the top by Hugill Hall. Turn **L** onto a road just after the farm and follow the track sharply **L** past the buildings. Climb on a walled track in the direction of Kentmere, passing a metalled lane on the right from Browfoot.

3 At the T-junction, turn **R** and continue until you reach two gates. Take the **RH** gate towards Kentmere Hall, following the bridleway alongside the wall. Eventually reach a gate in the wall and pass through it, continuing **SA** alongside the wall. Follow the bridleway to a gate, where the trail finally leaves walls and gates behind for a little while and climbs out across the fell. Follow this bold path and cross a stream to another gate.

4 Go through the gate and follow the bold path, hugging the wall, to the start of the ripping descent to Kentmere Hall. **Please** be aware of potential hazards on this descent: walkers, sheep and other mountain bikers climbing up. There are also a couple of gates, sometimes open, sometimes not. High speed can be achieved, but make sure you can stop or slow down in time.

5 The gate at Kentmere Hall is soon reached. Go through the gate and turn **R**, taking the farm track away from the hall. A short climb leads to the church and the road. Turn **L**. Follow the lane, bearing **L** at a fork (the right-hand option is closed with a gate). Continue for a short distance and turn **R** onto a wide, rocky track by a house – this is the Garburn Road.

6 After a brief effort you reach a gate. Continue through the gate to start the climb proper. How far can you get before exhaustion or the difficulty of the 'road' beats you? At the time of writing the pass was in the best condition for some years due to repair work and 4x4 bans. Hard men and women claim to be able to ride all the way to the top without dabbing. If this is your mindset then what are you waiting for? If you're **really** hard you could plant an axe in your head first!

7 After some effort – perhaps you walked bits perhaps you didn't (it really doesn't matter) – you reach the top gate. Continue through and the 'road' bears **L**, to another gate and the start of the descent. As with the descent to Kentmere Hall, be aware of other users climbing uphill. There are some tricky sections that can catch out even the best of riders so please take care!

8 At the bottom gate you have a choice: turn around and do the pass again, reversing the route back to Ings (recommended), or continue **SA** and finish quickly on tarmac. If continuing, follow the track through the gate to a fork. Take the **LH** (uphill) track, following it past Dubbs Reservoir on the right and down to the road.

9 Turn **L**, bearing **L** at the fork. Continue down the hill to a right-hand bend, a short climb and a drop down to the main road. Turn **L** and use the cycle path to return to Ings and a well-earned beverage.

Making a day of it

For starters, ride the route as a there and back – the pass is worth it. Then link it to the **Kentmere & Longsleddale** route on *page 69*.

FAST TRAILS ON BLACK COMBE

Black Combe

14km

Introduction

A real esoteric gem. Out on the coast, this great little hill gives spectacular views, weather permitting, out over the Irish Sea towards the Isle of Man and inland towards most of the Lakeland peaks. A testing climb on very good tracks up a 600m peak – no technical ability required just big thighs! The downhill is, as always, the reward for your hard work – on open fells with great views out to sea. Route finding is very easy on a clear day, but as Black Combe is on the coast, clouds can quickly amass around the summit. When this happens, the vague paths that are usually so easy to see in the distance all but disappear into the mist, so either take a compass or wait for a clear day.

The Ride

This route starts at Townend Hall on the A595 to give the legs a short warm-up, before the onslaught of Black Combe begins in earnest. From Whicham the bridleway kicks uphill to Black Combe. The riding is technically easy, but runs straight up a very big hill. Good tracks lead to the rounded summit with a shelter and trig point, from where the spectacular views can be admired. The path takes a close call to Blackcombe Screes before heading off downhill to Hall Foss, with distracting views out across the sea. A great bit of riding under Black Combe and parallel to the A595 leads back to Whitebeck and then on to your transport.

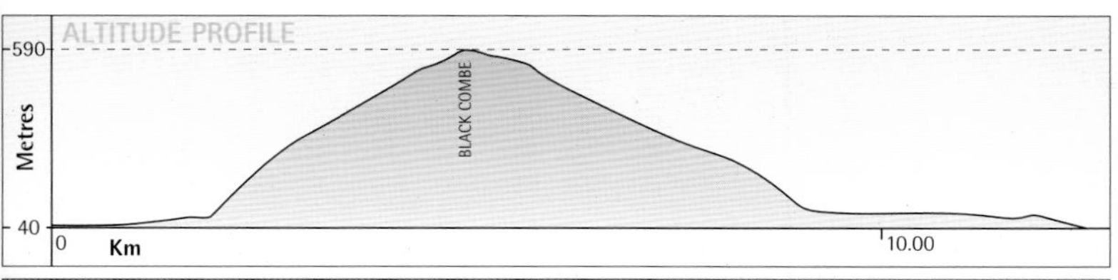

BLACK COMBE **GRADE: ▲**

DISTANCE: 14KM
TOTAL ASCENT: 681M
START/FINISH: TOWNEND HALL
GRID REFERENCE: SD 118 839
PARKING: LAYBY AT TOWNEND HALL
CAFÉ: NONE
PUBLIC HOUSE: PRINCE OF WALES, FOXFIELD Tel: 01229 716 238

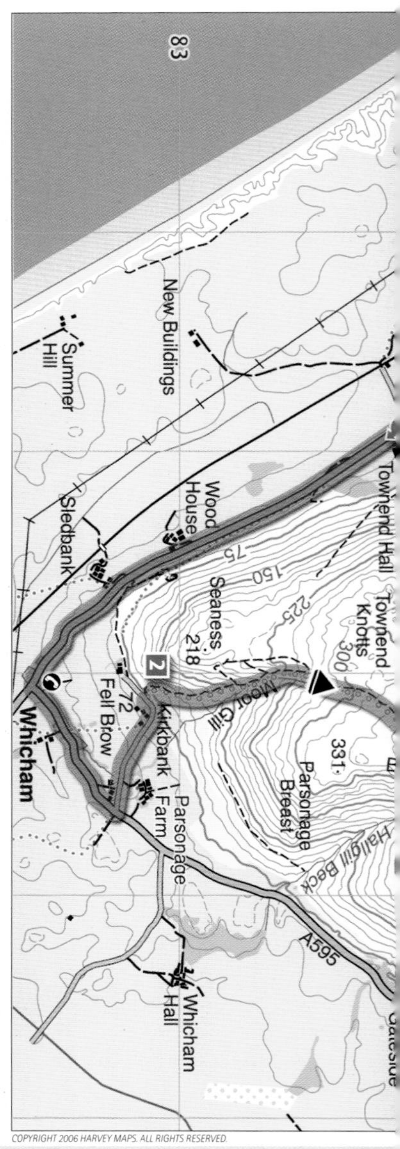
83
New Buildings
Summer Hill
Wood House
Sledbank
Townend Hall
Townend Knotts
300
Seaness
218
75
150
225
2
Moor Gill
331
Parsonage Breast
Hallgill Beck
A595
Fell Brow
72
Kirkbank Farm
Parsonage
Whicham
Whicham Hall

SD
Old Hyton
Holmegate
85
86
87
Gutterby
Millergill Beck
Stangrah
Barfield
Barfield Tarn
Broomhill
Far End
Holegill
13
14
15
16
Monk Foss Farm
Fell Cottage
Tarn Dimples
Long Crags
Monkfoss Beck
Holegill Beck
Hall Foss
Hallfoss Beck
Whitbeck
Little Fell
370
368
375
300
225
150
75
4
3
William Gill
450
525
Black Combe
600
587
485
Hentoe Hill
500
Hentoe Beck
Grassgill Beck
Great Grassoms
Blackcombe Screes
Whitecombe Screes
Anna Crag
Horse Back
Sty Knotts
Hallbeck Gill
Watery Crag
Crags
Black Combe

Directions – Black Combe

S From the lay-by at Townend Hall turn **L** onto the A595 to Whicham. At Whicham, follow the road to the **L**, signed *Broughton* (**ignore** the A5093 which continues straight ahead to Millom). After 700m, take the first **L** shortly after a layby up a small road, passing the old school and a church. After the last building the road turns to track. Bear **R** as the track splits shortly afterwards (straight ahead is a footpath). Ride to a gate and select your lowest gear...

2 The bridleway ahead is very good but very steep. The hardest section is the start up to Townend Knotts. Thereafter it is less steep (compared with what you have just ridden), but your legs are more tired so keep pumping. At the summit there is a trig point and a stone shelter – this can be a windy place with a stiff breeze coming in off the Irish Sea.

3 Continue **SA** over the summit on a vague track – if visibility is good there should be no problem – passing close to Blackcombe Screes on the right, before striking off to the **L** (north/north-west) and becoming more defined. **Ignore** the path going off right (north east) to Hentoe Hill, which is easily taken in poor conditions. It's vague and leads onto Whitecombe Screes – so if you are on near vertical scree slopes for a continued period you are off route!

4 A sheep-scattering descent across open fell eventually leads to a wall. Turn **L**, following the wall and fence. Ford the stream at Hall Foss, and the somewhat deeper stream at Holegill Beck. An undulating bridleway leads through to Whitebeck Mill and back to Townend Hall.

Making a day of it

This is a fairly isolated route, although it could be linked to the **Walna Scar** area if you're up for a lot of road riding.

AL SHELDON IN THE WOODS

Grizedale Loop

14.72km

Introduction

This is a short but cracking ride through Grizedale, taking in some of the highlights the forest has to offer in terms of natural trails. It's ideal as an evening ride, night-time ride or just a quick blast when time is limited. It will thrill you with the descents and have you reaching for your lowest gears on the climbs... go ride!

The Ride

Starting from Moor Top, the route maintains height on fire roads for a short while before heading down towards the centre of the forest. Not quite touching the visitor centre, it heads south towards Satterthwaite, where the route switches to the eastern side of the forest. Climbing steeply out of the village and you'll soon back in the forest on some fantastic singletrack leading into the superb Breasty Haw descent. Not over yet, the route climbs back into the forest after a brief spell on the black top. Fire roads and more singletrack return us to Moor Top.

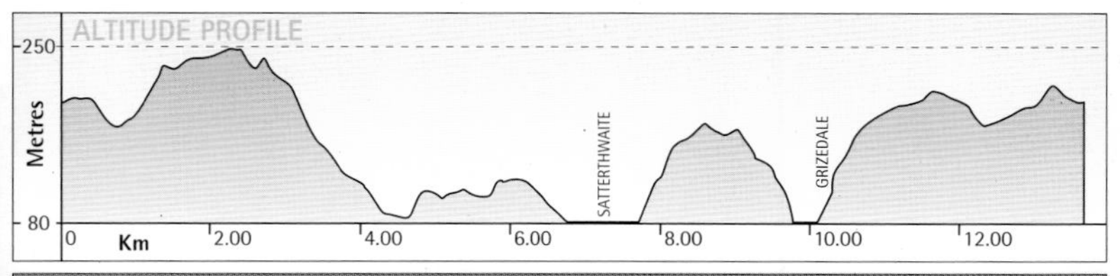

GRADE: ▲

DISTANCE: 14.72KM

TOTAL ASCENT: 517M

START/FINISH: MOOR TOP

GRID REFERENCE: SD 342 964

PARKING: MOOR TOP CAR PARK

CAFÉ: FORESTRY VISITOR CENTRE Tel: 01229 860 010

PUBLIC HOUSE: EAGLES HEAD, SATTERTHWAITE Tel: 01229 860 237

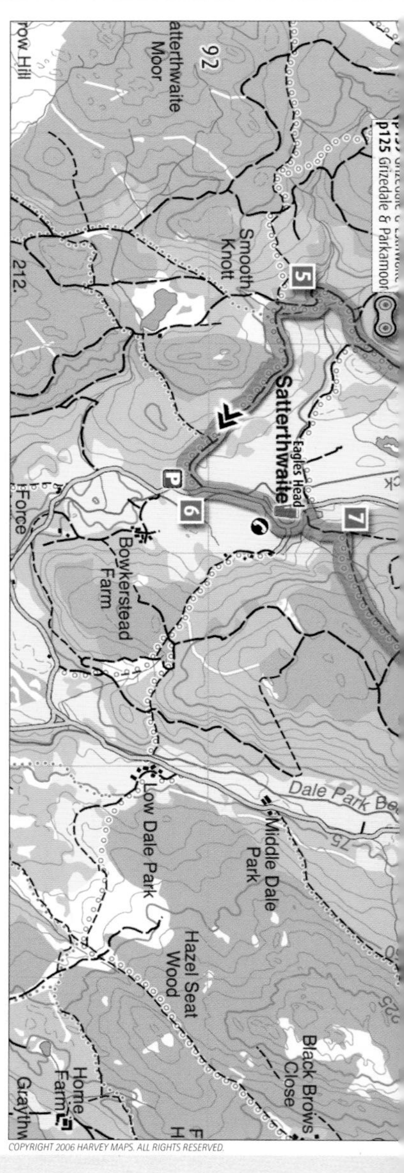
p125 Grizedale & Parkamoor
92
Smooth Knott
5
212.
Satterthwaite
Eagles Head
P
6
7
Force
Bowkerstead Farm
Low Dale Park
Middle Dale Park
Hazel Seat Wood
Black Brows Close
Home Farm

Grizedale Loop

Directions – Grizedale Loop

Note: *Some of the following directions refer to forest waymarks and signs. These can change frequently, so use the map and a bit of common sense if you can't spot something we've described. Grizedale is also a working forest – so obey any Forestry Commission signs you see!*

S From Moor Top car park take the exit leading into the forest. After passing the single bar gate, almost immediately bear **L** on a wide forest road signposted *Grizedale*. Keeping **L**, pass a turn on the left and bear **L** again, heading downhill. Continue to another sharp left-hand bend, immediately after crossing a stream.

2 Turn **R** uphill on a forest road. At the T-junction turn **L** to continue more gently uphill. A phone mast is up to your right on the horizon. Follow this undulating track for almost 1km. At the T-junction by a three-way waymark, turn **L**, signed *Parkamoor*. Turn immediately **L** again and shortly **L** for a third time, heading downhill on a rougher, steeper track.

3 From the junction a great descent follows with the occasional drop-off. Take it easy as walkers can be hidden around the corners or in the dips. The track pops you out on a wide forest road. Turn **R** downhill. Be aware of families on hire bikes – you are now very close to the visitor centre.

Optional Route

Easy to miss: Refreshment option just off the route at Grizedale Visitor Centre. After 550m of descent, turn sharp **L** back on yourself by wooden cycle-route signs to cross a cattle grid and descend to the centre and café.

4 Continue downhill to the bottom on the wide forest road, and two short climbs. **Ignoring** the bridleway joining on the left, continue climbing to a junction. Bear **L** down a short hill to a bridge with wooden railings either side.

5 Climb for 400m after the bridge, turning **L** as the gradient eases at the crossroads. Descend to cross a stream and climb to a gate. Take care once you're through the gate as the 1km descent to Satterthwaite gets narrow and rocky.

6 At the road, turn **L** towards the village. Pass the Eagles Head pub on the left. **Ignore** the road to the right just before the church and, on a left-hand bend, take the next road to the **R** between houses, climbing gently. Soon, at the T-junction of lanes, turn **R** again, climbing steeply uphill past Pepper House.

7 As the gradient eases, turn **R** opposite an isolated house on the left, on to a narrow stone track, signposted *Bridleway to High Dale Park*, to start an interesting climb back into the forest.

8 Did you clear everything on the way up? At the junction with the fire road, follow the bridleway **SA** to ride over Breasty Haw and drop to another fire road. Continue **SA** again. The descent which follows is one of the best in Grizedale with singletrack, drop offs and steep, off-camber corners!

9 At the T-junction with the minor road turn **L**. Climb the hill past a waterfall **ignoring** the bridleway on the right. At the top of a short climb turn **L** into a gravel car parking area and take the narrow stone bridleway climbing into the forest. The climb is quite steep in places, but otherwise straightforward. At the T-junction with the forest road turn **R**.

10 The fire road climbs slightly for 250m. On a sharp left-hand bend turn **R** onto the first forest road bridleway by some rocky outcrops. The trail winds its way through a landscape devastated by felling. The scenery improves upon re-entering woodland.

11 A last little climb leads to T-junction with a forest road. Turn **R** down the hill, soon passing 'The Fox', a famous forest landmark, as you round a left-hand bend. Turn **R** on the bend and then turn **L** onto a bridleway. The more obvious track to the right is for another day!

12 The bridleway drops down through the trees, eventually emerging on a fire road. Once there, turn **L**. Follow the fire road uphill, eventually you will reach a track T-junction, turn **R** and drop down to the road. Turn **R**, then after 200m, **L** into Moor Top car park.

Making a day of it

Try the man-made singletrack **TNF Trail** from the main visitor centre in the forest, or just go and explore – the forest is full of great trails.

BEGINNING THE FAST DESCENT TO KESWICK

Two Routes form Keswick

19.5km or 16.5km

Introduction

Keswick is the only big(ish) town in the Northern Lakes. It's easy to reach, has a bike shop, pubs, cafés and a pencil museum. As a result, lots of people head there, which can cause problems with parking (there are at least two other car parks along this route if you can't find a space in Keswick) and may mean annoyingly busy trails. Don't worry – these routes are still worth doing. They are both relatively short, so early morning or evening bashes are a real possibility. The Lonscale Fell Loop is a relatively easy offering for the northern Lakes. It involves only a little technical riding and is great fun. The Skiddaw route is slightly different. Look north from Keswick. See that enormous hill? Now carry your bike up it and slide back down.

The Ride

The Lonscale Fell Loop leaves Keswick along the old railway line, crossing some massive north shore stuff (tongue firmly in cheek) on the way. Steep road work gets most of the climbing out of the way before a track runs up into the hills. Things get technical as you descend to ford Glendeterra beck, and you'll be doing well if you ride the return leg in one. Technical singletrack leads back down the valley to a fast descent (walkers permitting) into Keswick.

To tackle Skiddaw, grind up and out of Keswick. From there you'll probably manage to ride for about another kilometre before you're off and pushing. Carry/push/ride – whatever you can manage – to the top and then tackle the loose stone descent at whatever speed you feel happy with.

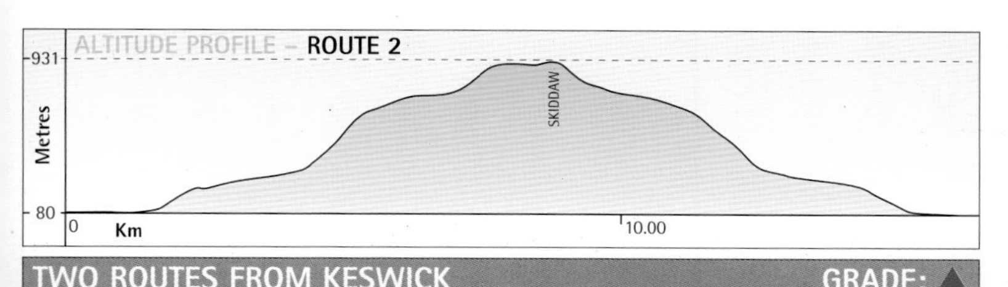

TWO ROUTES FROM KESWICK — **GRADE:** ▲

DISTANCE: 19.5 (ROUTE 1) OR 16.5KM (ROUTE 2)

START/FINISH: KESWICK TOWN CENTRE

PARKING: PAY AND DISPLAY IN KESWICK

PUBLIC HOUSE: TAKE YOUR PICK IN KESWICK

TOTAL ASCENT: 400 (ROUTE 1) OR 925M (ROUTE 2)

GRID REFERENCE: NY 266 236

CAFÉ: LOTS OF CHOICE

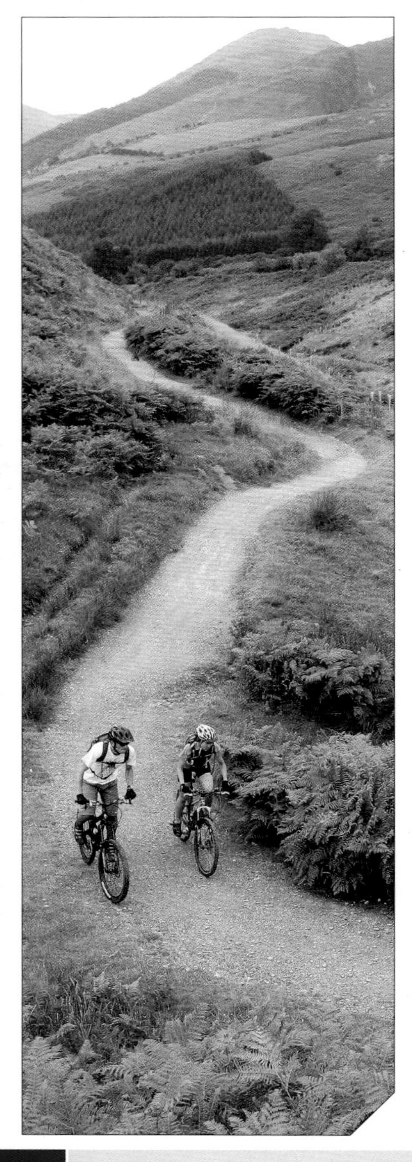

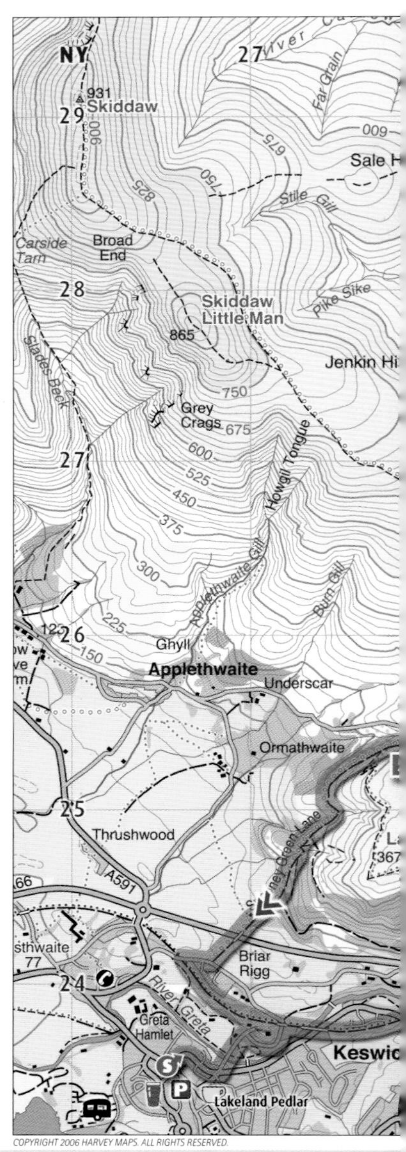
NY
27
931
Skiddaw
29
900
825
750
675
600
Far Grain
Sale H
Stile Gill
Carside Tarn
Broad End
28
Skiddaw Little Man
865
Pike Sike
Jenkin Hi
Slades Beck
750
Grey Crags
675
600
525
450
375
300
225
150
Howgil Tongue
Applethwaite Gill
Burn Gill
27
26
Ghyll
Applethwaite
Underscar
Ormathwaite
25
Thrushwood
A591
Briar Rigg
24
River Greta
Greta Hamlet
Keswic
Lakeland Pedlar
77
66
367

Two Routes From Keswick (Route 1)

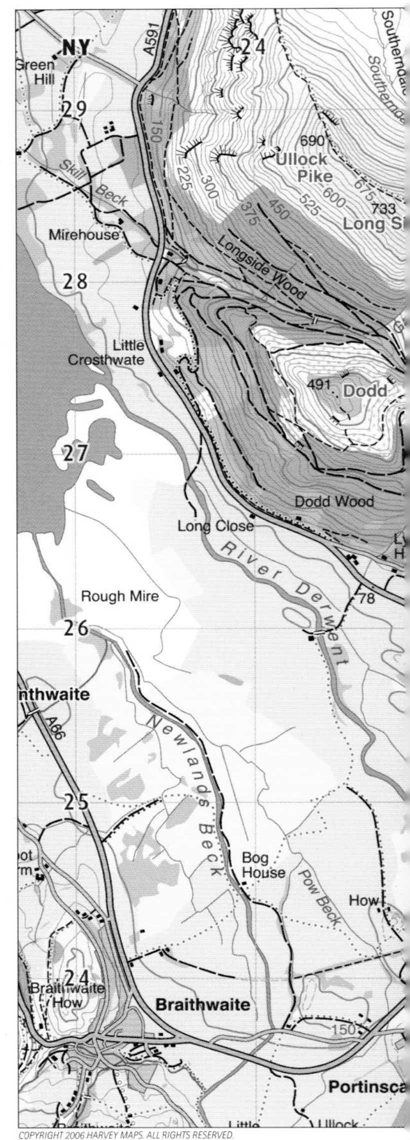

NY
A591
Green Hill
29
24
Southernmost
690
Ullock Pike
733
Long S
Skill Beck
Mirehouse
150
225
300
375
450
525
600
675
Longside Wood
28
Little Crosthwate
491
Dodd
27
Dodd Wood
Long Close
River Derwent
78
Rough Mire
26
nthwaite
A66
Newlands Beck
25
Bog House
Pow Beck
How
24
Braithwaite How
Braithwaite
150
Portinsca

Two Routes From Keswick (Route 2)

Directions – Two Routes From Keswick

Route 1: Lonscale Fell Loop – 19.5km

S From the long-stay car park behind Keswick Mountain Bikes, go back out onto the main road and turn **L**. Turn **L** onto Station Road just after the pedestrian crossing (traffic lights), and follow the road to a mini roundabout. Turn **L** into the leisure centre car park and, once in the car park, **L** again onto the old railway line, signed *Keswick Railway Footpath*. Follow this out of the car park and continue **SA** along it for around 5km.

2 At the main road, turn **L** and then **L** again shortly afterwards, towards Threlkeld. Ride into the village, taking the second **L**, signed *Blease Road Leading to Blencathra*.

3 Climb up the lane **ignoring** all turnings, until you reach the Blencathra Centre. Keep **R** and ride **SA** through a small car park onto a wide stone bridleway, signed *Skiddaw House*. Follow the obvious track up the valley. At the valley head, follow the track to the left, descend to ford the river and then climb to a bridleway T-junction.

4 Turn **L** to climb back along the western side of the valley. Tricky riding (watch the drop...) leads through a gate to an easier track. Follow this to pass through two more gates. Turn **R** just after the second gate, through a third into a small car park.

5 Turn **L** through a gate at the far side of the car park. (A sign on the gate warns cyclists of the drainage ditches.) This track can be busy, so take care. Bear **R** at the fork and descend around switchbacks. Keep **R** at the next fork, go **SA** through the gate and turn **L** at the road. Ride to the mini roundabout and re-trace your outward route.

Route 2: Skiddaw – 16.5km

S From the long-stay car park behind Keswick Mountain Bikes, go back out onto the main road and turn **L**. Turn **L** onto Station Road just after the pedestrian crossing (traffic lights), and follow the road to a mini roundabout.

2 Turn **R** and follow the road past houses for 300m before turning **R** onto an obvious bridleway.

3 **Ignoring** all turnings, climb to a gate leading into a car park. Turn **R** through the car park, turning **L** immediately beyond the gate at the far end. Pass through two more gates and bear **L** at the fork just after the second.

4 Climb!

5 Stick to the obvious track, climbing continuously until you reach the summit. Take a breather and then re-trace your steps (at a considerably higher speed) to your car.

Making a day of it

Either of these short routes can be added into the **Skiddaw Loop** on *page 145*. The Lonscale Fell loop in particular makes a great alternative start to this longer ride.

LEAVING SANDWICK

Ullswater Singletrack

18km

Introduction

For the technically able, this is an awesome little ride. Using mainly stone-based tracks, it's also a fairly all-weather loop, although it can get a little boggy higher up. You might want to choose a different route on a sunny Sunday, as the superb track alongside Ullswater (the highlight of the ride) can get crowded with walkers. Never climbing to the high fell-tops that characterise many routes in the north Lakes, the route avoids forcing you off the bike for a long portage. Don't under-estimate it or make the mistake of deciding it's an easy ride though: there's still a (very) steep climb to be conquered; and the wide stone singletrack along Ullswater that seems tantalisingly doable – and yet often proves to be a little too technical to be cleaned.

The Ride

A quick spin along the road takes you onto a bridleway through fields at Bridgend. Cross the river onto a wide stone track and head steeply uphill, climbing 200 metres in just over a kilometre. Take a breather(!) at the top and admire the views out across the valley towards Helvellyn. Cross the plateau on vague trails and pick up the fast and swoopy singletrack descent into Martindale and onto tarmac. Roll down the road to a short grassy bridleway and then on to Sandwick. A grassy bridleway just before the car park starts innocently enough, soon becoming rocky and heading downhill before turning into a mega-technical undulating trail running along the shore of Ullswater. If you can clean this, you're doing well!

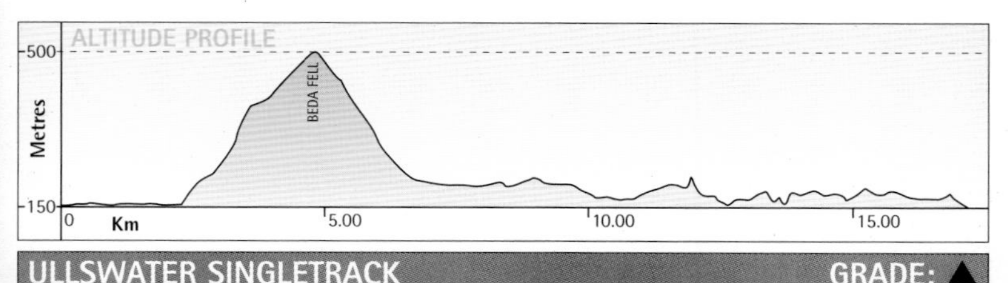

ULLSWATER SINGLETRACK — **GRADE: ▲**

DISTANCE: 18KM

START/FINISH: CAR PARK IN PATTERDALE

PARKING: PAY AND DISPLAY IN PATTERDALE

PUBLIC HOUSE: THE NEAREST IS IN GLENRIDDING

TOTAL ASCENT: 720M

GRID REFERENCE: NY 395 159

CAFÉ: NONE

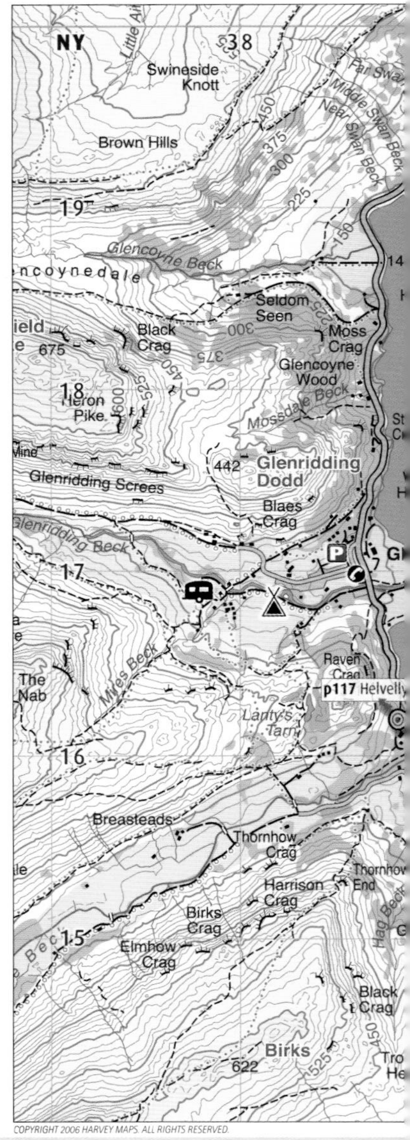

NY
38
Swineside Knott
Brown Hills
Middle Swan Beck
Near Swan Beck
450
375
300
225
150
19
Glencoyne Beck
Seldom Seen
Black Crag
675
300
375
Moss Crag
Glencoyne Wood
18
Heron Pike
600
525
450
Mossdale Beck
442
Glenridding Dodd
Glenridding Screes
Blaes Crag
Glenridding Beck
17
Raven Crag
p117 Helvelly
The Nab
Miles Beck
Lanty's Tarn
16
Breasteads
Thornhow Crag
Harrison Crag
Birks Crag
Elmhow Crag
15
Hag Beck
Black Crag
Birks
622
525
450

Ullswater Singletrack
Steamer Service to Glenridding
Ullswater
40
41
42
43
A592
Aira Point
Bay
Sandwick
Sandwick Beck
Waterc
388
Hallin Fell
St. Peter's Church
6
Long Crag
377
Scalehow Force
Kilbert How
Scalehow Beck
Cat Crag
Sleet Fell
378
Garth Head
Birk Fell
High Dodd
501
Nettleslack
Winter Crag
5
196
Howegrain Beck
Silver Hill
Mortar Crag
Black Crag
Boredale Beck
Raven Crag
The Knight
525
Martindale
Beda Head
509
Thrang Crag
Boardale Head
657
Place Fell
600
450
375
300
225
Hawk Crag
Beda Fell
Round How
Redgate Gill
Boardale
Dalehead
7
Patterdale
Rooking Gill
Bedafell Knott
Red Scar
Blue Gill
4
Goldrill Bridge
Chapel in the Hause
393
Boarddale Hause
Mill Moss
Stonebarrow Gill
531
Crookabeck
3
Bannerdale Beck
Rake Crag
Heck Cove
Heck Beck
Arnison Crag
Goldrill Beck
Stoney Rigg
Freeze Beck
577
The Nab
Beckstones
Heck Crag
Angletarn Pikes
567
Bannerdale
Dubhow Crag
Dubhow Beck
2
Bridgend
Yewgrove
Dubhow Gill
Dubhow
p153 High Street North
Fall Crag
Cat Crag

Directions – Ullswater Singletrack

S Leave Patterdale on the A592, heading south, away from Ullswater towards the Kirkstone Pass. After 1.8km, turn **L** onto a signed bridleway, just before the last house in Bridgend. If you reach a red phone box on the right, you've gone too far.

2 Follow the bridleway through gates and fields, crossing the river and meeting a wide track. Turn **R** and then sharply back **L** after a short distance to climb steeply up a wide track towards Boardale Hause.

3 After a very steep section the gradient eases as the track swings to the right and reaches a plateau. Head for the ridge on the east side of the plateau. **Ignoring** obvious tracks to the left and right, the bridleway heads **L** at a 45° angle on a vague grassy trail, before cutting back **R** and up to the ridge. As you reach the far side of the plateau, the track swings left (north) as it climbs up onto the ridge and turns to perfect singletrack.

4 Summiting the ridge, go **SA** over a crossroads of narrow tracks (bearing slightly to the **R** and then back **L** as you start to descend). Awesome singletrack descent into Martindale. Stick to the 'main' track all the way (anything else is a sheep track). Pick up the road at the buildings at Dalehead and follow it down the valley.

5 Turn **L** onto a grassy bridleway just before a farm and a bridge. Follow it to the road and turn **L** (**SA** in effect). Descend round a hairpin, following signs for Sandwick. Turn **L** immediately before the car park onto a bridleway signed Bridleway to Patterdale.

6 The track turns to technical singletrack which undulates along the side of Ullswater. Stick to the main obvious track and **ignore** all turnings. The track eventually widens after a final climb and becomes a well-made track.

7 Go **SA** through the gate at Side Farm and **SA** through the next gate onto tarmac. Follow the road round to the right and out to Patterdale.

Making a day of it

This route is right beside the **High Street North ride** *(see page 153)*, and adds a little technical spice to that route.

FRED YONG AND PETE DODDS HEADING FOR THE SINGLETRACK

LAKELAND RIVER CROSSING

Seathwaite – Dunnerdale

18km

Introduction

For those based in the West of the Lake District, this represents a classic ride, taking in superb undulating terrain. Apart from a steep section at the start of the Walna Scar Road and an exposed start to one of the downhills, this is an amenable ride. Although this route shares parts with Walna Scar, the Dunnerdale Valley doesn't attract the crowds found on the other side of the hill, but still contains great riding. Route finding can be tricky sometimes due to the number of (or lack of) trails and vague trails, so take a compass.

The Ride

Starting in Seathwaite the ride heads north-east to the start of the Walna Scar Road. At the time of writing, 4x4s are banned on this track, but this may change. A grind up the hill is inevitable, but soon rewarded by a great downhill through the quarries into the boglands and a superb technical downhill singletrack. Don't feel too sorry for any bikers you meet coming up – they're no doubt heading for the awesome descent down the Walna Scar road. After passing through Stephenson Ground, contour around Raven's Crag and over to the Dunnerdale Fells. Good singletrack eventually leads to the Dunnerdale Valley, wide farm tracks take you to Kiln Bank Farm and then road takes you back to Seathwaite.

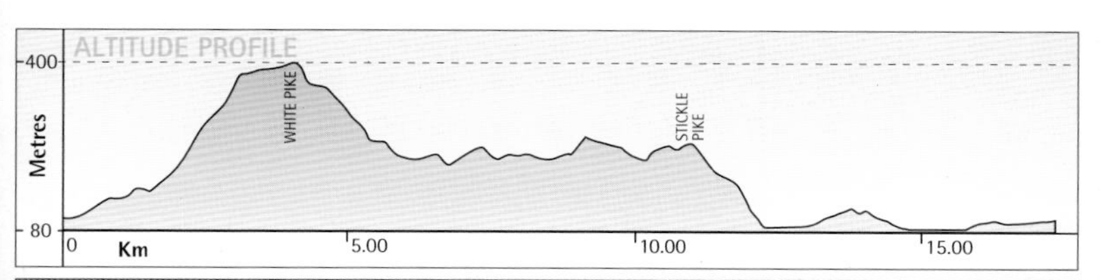

SEATHWAITE – DUNNERDALE **GRADE: ▲**

DISTANCE: 18KM
TOTAL ASCENT: 443M
START/FINISH: SEATHWAITE
GRID REFERENCE: SD 229 962
PARKING: LAYBY OPPOSITE SMALL CHAPEL
CAFÉ: NEWFIELD INN, SEATHWAITE Tel: 01229 716 208
PUBLIC HOUSE: NEWFIELD INN, SEATHWAITE Tel: 01229 716 208

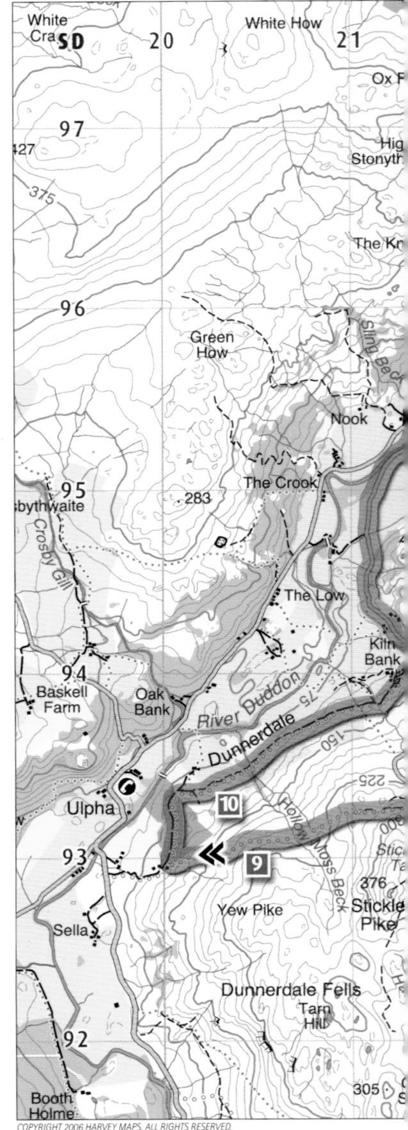
White Crag
SD
20
White How
21
97
427
375
96
Green How
Nook
The Crook
95
283
Crosby Gill
The Low
Kiln Bank
94
Baskell Farm
Oak Bank
River Duddon
Dunnerdale
Ulpha
10
9
93
Hollow Moss Beck
Yew Pike
376
Stickle Pike
Sella
Dunnerdale Fells
Tarn Hill
92
305
Booth Holme

Seathwaite –
Dunnerdale
Seathwaite
Newfield Inn
Tongue House
Long House
Long House Gill
Walna Scar Road
p161 Walna Scar
White Pike
White Maiden
Brown Pike
Turner Hall Farm
Moss Crag
Wash Dub Beck
Gobling Beck
High Greens
Pikes
Caw
Natty Bridge
Broughton Moor Quarry
p93 Broughton Moor & Seathwaite
Fox Haw
Stephenson Ground
Jackson Ground
Raven's Crag
Carter Ground
Ball Hall
The Knott
Knott End
River Lickle
Appletree Worth Beck
Town End
Wallbarrow Gorge
Hollin How
Hollin House Tongue
Peel Crag
Seathwaite Buttress
Low Crag
Old Park Beck
Tarn Beck

Directions – Seathwaite – Dunnerdale

S From the lay-by opposite the chapel, turn **L** along the road. At the fork, bear **R**, signed *Coniston, Unfit For Cars* (that's OK – you're on your bike!). After a short distance, fork **R** onto a bridleway signed *Walna Scar*, passing through a gate and past *Road Closed* signs (these are for the 4x4s). Now the adventure starts.

2 You can see the big wide trail ahead. Fortunately you don't have to go all the way to the top, only to the second wall. The track may take some pushing, but is over surprisingly quickly.

3 At the wall with the gate and bar, turn **R** immediately beyond the gate, passing under slag heaps and following the wall until the bridleway joins a trail coming in from the left. Continue **SA** through the old quarries.

4 **Easy to miss:** The route becomes vague through boggy terrain and there are a number of false paths. Aim to pass to the right of a craggy knoll – where all tracks seem to join. Descend via technical singletrack. **Ignore** the turning left over Natty Bridge onto a wide trail down the left-hand side of the valley. Follow the track heading **SA** for the **RH** bank of the River Lickle for an awesome singletrack descent. Exposed at first with steep banking into the river, the singletrack then becomes an exciting bit of technical riding, which ends at Stephenson Ground.

5 Turn **R** in front of the gate, onto a bridleway signed *Seathwaite*. Follow this north-west, climbing steeply beside a wall and crossing the stream. Follow the track between walls by the stream, passing through a second gated wall to a 3-way junction.

6 Turn **L** and continue downhill by the wall, bearing **L** at the fork. Continue across the sometimes-boggy ground to take a circuitous route to Jackson Ground. Undulating terrain takes you towards Raven's Crag. **Ignore** the bridleway on the left and climb, steeply towards the end, on to the ridge.

7 As the bridleway levels, bear **R** at the fork and descend (does the joy never end?) until you come to a crossroads with a big track. Continue **SA** over this track onto a steep bridleway which climbs to Kiln Bank Cross.

8 **Easy to miss:** Turn **R** onto the road and head downhill. 10m before a cattle grid sign, turn **L** onto a vague trail, which becomes more obvious after a short boggy section. The trail follows the wall for a good distance, before fording the beck and bearing **R** on a now good bridleway to a bridleway sign.

9 The track becomes vague once more. Bear **R** and head downhill towards the forest, soon picking up the trail once more and heading steeply downhill to the road beside a house. Turn **R** and go through a gate into Birks Wood.

10 Fork **R** just after leaving the woods – do not continue **SA** as it is a private track. Pleasant tracks lead to Kiln Bank Farm and the road. Turn **L** and steeply downhill – beware of cars as the road is narrow. Follow the road alongside the River Duddon back to Seathwaite and refreshments.

Making a day of it

Turn south down the road after Raven's Crag and pick up the bridleway running from Broughton Mills into Dunnerdale for a stiff climb and excellent singletrack descent.

top 10
Climbs
Some climbs are steep. Some are technical.
The best are both! See how many of these climbs
you can conquer – no dabbing now...

1 Moor Howe to Garburn Pass Summit (Garburn Pass) GR NY 423 006 – 435 044

Some quite technical sections as you start to tire.

2 Kiln Bank Cross to Raven Crag (Broughton Moor) GR SD 214 932 – 224 922

Looks impossible but in fact gives in quite easily to strong legs!

3 Miterdale Head to Tongue Moor (Miterdale & Eskdale) GR NY 159 025 – 173 036

Bit of a push to get going, then it's just a matter of how high you want your heart to go.

4 Sadgill to Cocklaw Fell (Longsleddale & Kentmere) GR NY 483 057 – 479 049

Take a break at the river before you grind your way up this one. After the gate where the bridleway divides is a special challenge – some steep, technical ground; gold star if you get up!

5 A593/Arnside – Iron Keld (Iron Keld and Loughrigg GR NY 335 029 – 337 011

From the A593 this steep bridleway grinds away through reasonably technical terrain.

High Tilberthwaite GR NY 307 014 – 308 023

Short, steep and rocky. Might take more than one attempt, but completely do-able.

Low Bank Ground to Lawson Park (Grizedale & Esthwaite) GR SD 315 968 – 322 950

The reverse of the downhill, this time the gates give a welcome rest.

Black Combe (Black Coombe) GR SD 131 827 – 134 855

A real leg burner; the start is very steep, so maybe try to save your legs. Nowhere technical – it's all good tracks – it's just very steep.

Skiddaw House (Skiddaw) GR NY 249 323 – 272 313

Climb the broad track from Peter House Farm. Technically easy, but with a steep bit just before the gate.

Robin Lane to Hundreds Road (Jenkin Crag & Troutbeck) GR NY 407 026 – 397 023

A good beginners' climb on which to see if the legs are up to more arduous work.

SECTION 2

Epics

Getting longer now – these loops will take a bit more time and effort. Not rides to be scared of, but definitely rides to be respected. Rather large hills and plenty of technical ground to cover mean that firstly, you're going to be out for a good few hours and secondly, you're going to have a really good time.

Epics route finder

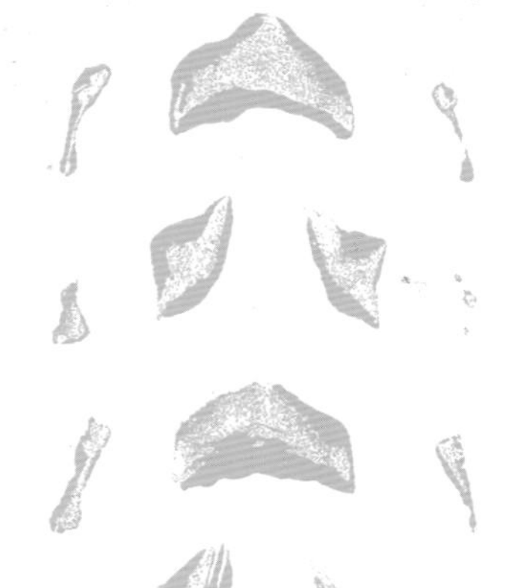

Maryport
A594
A595
Cocker
A66
WORKINGTON
A597
A596
A595
A595
Loweswater
WHITEHAVEN
A5086
Crummock Water
B5295
B5295
Ennerdale Water
B5345
LAK
Wast Water
B5343
A595
0 miles 4
0 km 5
N
B530

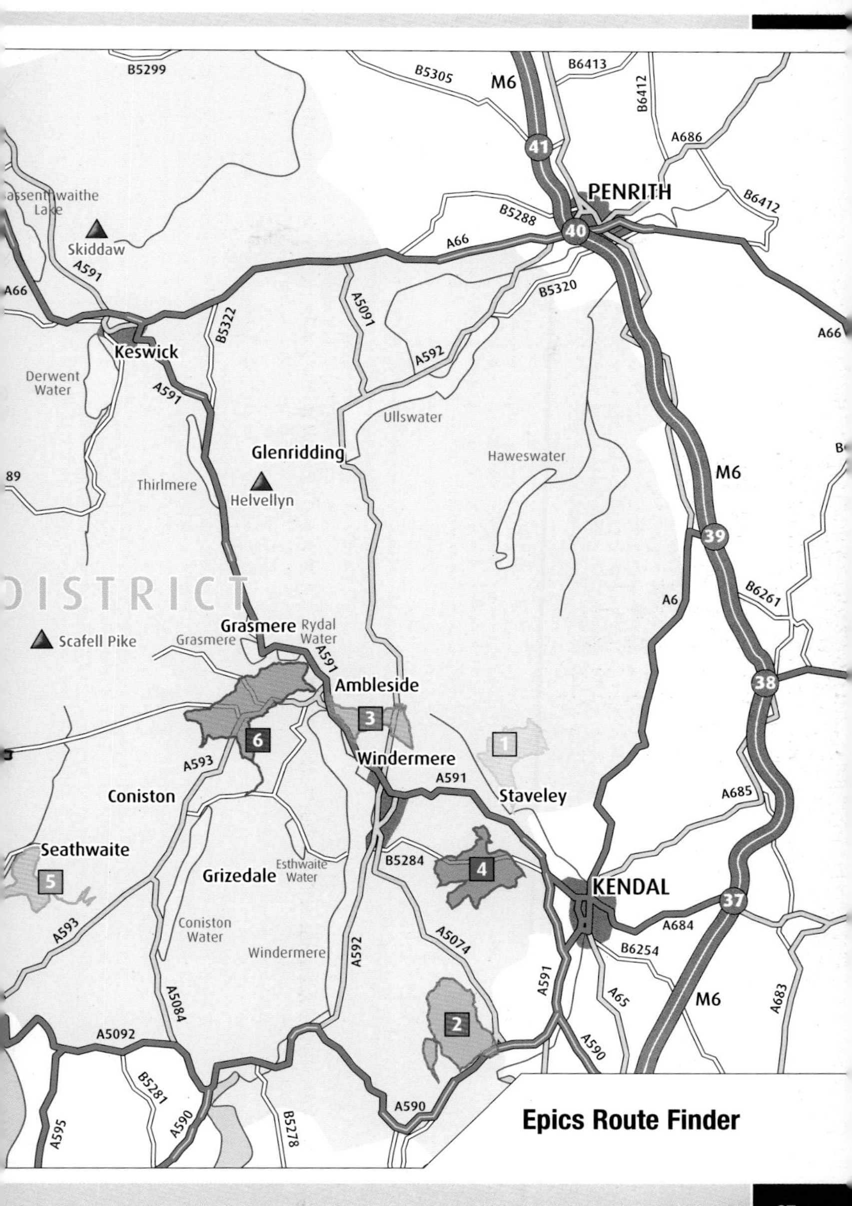
B5299
B5305
M6
B6413
B6412
A686
41
PENRITH
B6412
B5288
40
Skiddaw
A591
A66
A66
B5320
A5091
B5322
A66
Keswick
A592
Derwent Water
A591
Ullswater
Glenridding
Haweswater
M6
Thirlmere
Helvellyn
39
DISTRICT
B6261
A6
Grasmere
Rydal Water
Scafell Pike
Grasmere
A591
38
Ambleside
3
1
6
A593
Windermere
A591
Coniston
Staveley
A685
Seathwaite
B5284
4
5
Grizedale
Esthwaite Water
KENDAL
37
A593
Coniston Water
A5074
A684
B6254
Windermere
A592
A591
A65
M6
A683
A5084
2
A5092
A590
B5281
A590
A590
B5278
A595
Epics Route Finder

Kentmere & Longsleddale

23km

Introduction

Another classic ride in the Kentmere valley, looping anticlockwise over into Longsleddale and back again. This route gives a great introduction to Lake District riding without having to travel into the heart of the Lakes, thus avoiding both the crowds and the journey time. The riding on the east side of the valley can feel very remote, even though it's so close to the village of Staveley. It's worth noting that this side of the valley can be quite boggy after continued rain, so choose your day carefully. Kentmere is a great area for the novice biker looking to become a bit more adventurous, or for those wanting to start and end their ride at a great café.

The Ride

This ride takes you to the quiet and picturesque valley of Longsleddale. Leaving Staveley on metalled roads, it's not long before a track takes you onto the open fells of Kentmere. There are many alternative bridleways in this area, but this route follows the well-worn track leading to Green Quarter. After some good singletrack the ride breaks off right on ill-defined bridleways to Longsleddale, where the vague tracks give way to a solid trail and a great downhill. Spin up the valley on tarmac and a good trail climbs over to Green Quarter, from where you'll soon find yourself in the picturesque village of Kentmere. From here it's uphill on good tracks to Whiteside End and a rest for your legs on the downhills that follow, taking you all the way back to the start.

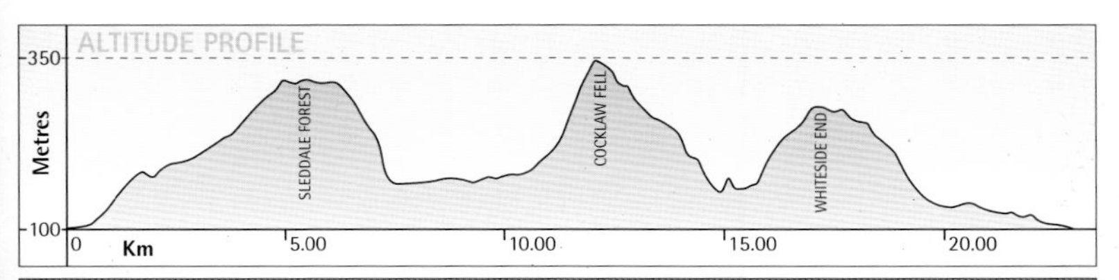

KENTMERE & LONGSLEDDALE — **GRADE:** ▲

DISTANCE: 23KM

START/FINISH: STAVELEY WOOD MILL YARD

PARKING: STAVELEY WOOD MILL YARD

PUBLIC HOUSE: EAGLE & CHILD, STAVELEY Tel: 01539 821 320

TOTAL ASCENT: 704M

GRID REFERENCE: SD 470 982

CAFÉ: WILF'S Tel: 01539 822 329

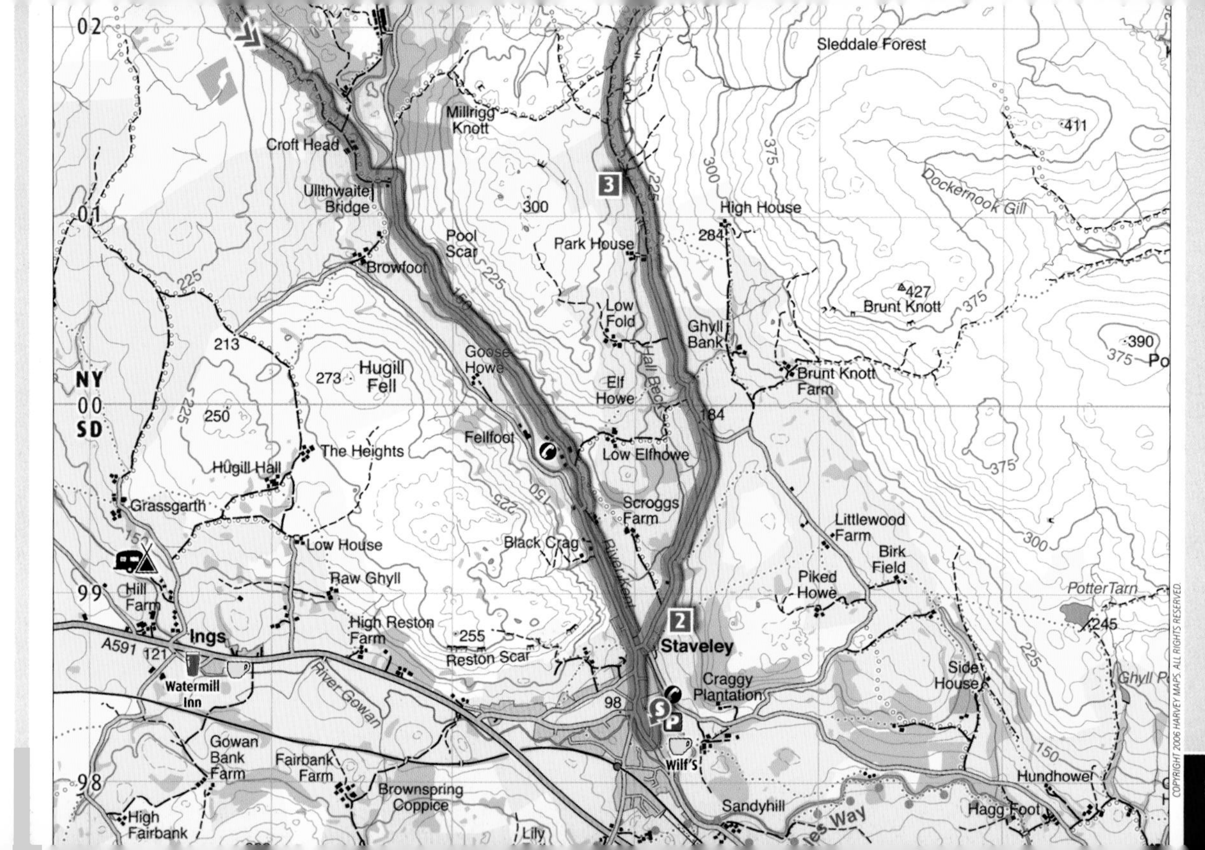

02
01
NY
00
SD
99
98
Sleddale Forest
Millrigg Knott
Croft Head
Ullthwaite Bridge
300
3
High House
Dockernook Gill
411
375
Pool Scar
Park House
284
Browfoot
225
427
Brunt Knott
Low Fold
Ghyll Bank
213
390
Hugill Fell
273
Goose Howe
Brunt Knott Farm
Elf Howe
Hall Beck
250
184
Fellfoot
The Heights
Low Elfhowe
Hugill Hall
Grassgarth
Scroggs Farm
Littlewood Farm
Low House
Black Crag
River Kent
Birk Field
Piked Howe
Raw Ghyll
Hill Farm
Potter Tarn
2
245
High Reston Farm
Ings
255
Staveley
A591
121
Reston Scar
Side House
Craggy Plantation
Watermill Inn
River Gowan
98
Gowan Bank Farm
Fairbank Farm
Wilf's
Brownspring Coppice
Hundhowe
Sandyhill
Hagg Foot
High Fairbank
Lily
150

Kentmere & Longsleddale

Directions – Kentmere & Longsleddale

S Turn **R** out of the car park onto Back Lane, and then **R** again at the main Kentmere road, heading north-west.

2 Turn **R** over Barley Bridge (weir), then immediately **L** to climb up Hall Lane. Continue **SA**, climbing quite steeply in parts, until you reach Park End (Park House on the map). Continue **SA** onto a farm track, which gradually opens out.

3 Follow the wall, **ignoring** bridleway(s) on the left, until the track takes you away from the wall and through a gate. Bear **R** (bridleway sign) at the fork, heading north-east (the left fork is not a bridleway). The trail continues uphill on some great singletrack that feels as though it's in a shallow ravine. **Easy to miss**: as you exit the ravine, the trail forks by a cairn. Take the vague trail to the **R**.

4 Continue **SA**, heading for a gate in a wall. Go through the gate, over a footbridge and follow the trail, heading roughly east, through some fine scenery with a great sense of seclusion and remoteness.

5 Eventually a final gate leads to a descent that swings left and north into Longsleddle. At the end of the downhill, go through the **RH** of the two gates by the cottages (Valley View and Spring Cottage) onto a signed bridleway. Continue downhill and follow the track out to Wadshowe Bridge and the road. **NB.** You can take the bridleway that turns left past the cottages to Till's Hole, but this is generally hard work and can be very boggy.

6 Turn **L** along the road and head north to Sadgill. **Ignore** the first bridleway to Kentmere at Till's Hole (after 2km) and continue another 800m, following the road over a bridge (the track running straight ahead is Gatesgarth Pass leading to Haweswater). Once over the bridge turn **L** at bridleway sign then **R** in front of the farm to another gate.

7 Climb gradually through Sadgill Woods (heading south) to a gate. Once through this gate, **ignore** the bridleway to the left and continue **SA** up the steep track in front of you (this is a good technical downhill, but unfortunately you're going up it!). The track eventually plateaus and a fun downhill (with a few gates) follows.

8 Join the road (High Lane) and turn **L** towards Kentmere. After a gate and a fast downhill, take the first road on your **R** (goes back acutely) and descend to Low Bridge. Turn **R** towards Kentmere church. Just before the church, turn **L** onto the bridleway (on tarmac initially) to Kentmere Hall.

9 Follow the track **SA** through the gate and round to the left, where the uphill struggle starts, albeit on good trails – so no getting off here apart from the gates! At the top, the trail swings to the right and downhill, enjoy. After short steep downhill section the track swings back left and through a gate.

10 Immediately beyond the gate, the bridleway forks. Bear **L** (do not ford the stream), for an exhilarating downhill. Follow this through Croft Head to Ullthwaite Bridge. Go over the bridge and turn **R** along the Kentmere road for an easy spin back to Wilf's for your cake and tea.

Making a day of it

Continue over the Gurburn Pass from Kentmere.

Whitbarrow Scar

21.5km

Introduction

This is a two-hour-plus ride on the edge of the Lake District National Park. Passing through some beautiful, semi-natural woodland, this is a route which throws up a few surprises that will have you screaming for more!

The Ride

The route starts from Raven's Lodge, and from the moment you leave tarmac, starts to climb below White Scar. From the top, the bridleway drops down to Mill Side where we take a sharp right in the direction of Witherslack Hall School and Equestrian Centre. From here, after a brief interlude on tarmac, the route heads into the woods for a rollercoaster descent into Witherslack village. Pounding blacktop for a couple of kilometres soon sees us off-road again, this time on a challenging climb back up to Witherslack Hall. Turning left the route follows the quiet lane to Broad Oak where another challenging climb is rewarded with a 'how-fast-can-I-go' downhill. From the end of which we join the A5074 for the ride back to the car.

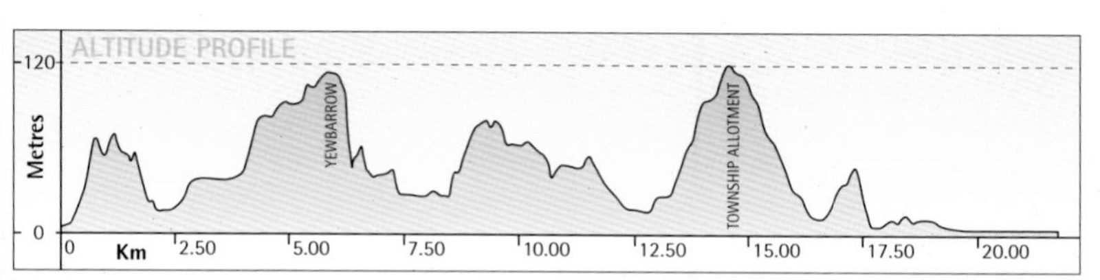

WHITBARROW SCAR **GRADE: ▲**

DISTANCE: 21.5KM
TOTAL ASCENT: 502M
START/FINISH: RAVEN'S LODGE
GRID REFERENCE: SD 462 851
PARKING: ON OLD A590 AT THE HEAD OF THE LANE TO RAVEN'S LODGE
CAFÉ: NONE ON ROUTE
PUBLIC HOUSE: GILPIN BRIDGE INN, GILPIN BRIDGE Tel: 01539 552 206

Witherslack Hall Farm
Lawns Wood
Askew Green
Strickland Hill
Moss Howe
Yewbarrow
Hell Moss
Key Moss
Slate Hill
Holme
Halecat House
High Fell End
Bowes Lodge
Longhowe End
Low Green
Nichols Wood
Sunny Green
Catcragg
Birks
Nether Hall
Witherslack
Town End
Beck Head Farm
Kirket Nook
Mill Side
Low Fell End
Bowgreave Busk
Low Crag Wood
High Crag Wood
Chapel Head Scar
Buckhouse Wood
Whitbarrow Lodge
Farrer's Allotment
White Scar
Rawsons
Rawson's Wood
Gilpin Farm
Gilpin House
Raven's Lodge
Main Drain
Sampool Plain
Stakes Moss
A590
A5074
High Foulshaw
Summer Hill
Foulshaw Moss
Middle Foulshaw
2
3
4
5
6
7
10

Whitbarrow Scar

Directions – Whitbarrow Scar

S Ride down the lane towards the farm. As soon as you pass the farm entrance on the right, turn **L** through a gate, passing a cowshed. Continue through the next gate onto the first climb.

2 Climb through the wood, sticking to the bridleway, until it eventually tops out and exits the wood, soon joining an unmade road by a gateway. Turn **R**, heading away from the gateway. The lane soon turns to tarmac, heading downhill quite steeply and passing a farm on the left.

3 At the bottom of the hill do not continue to the road junction, but turn sharp **R** (almost back on yourself) in the direction of Beck Head.

4 After 750m, this lane turns to an unmade track by some cottages. Continue **SA**, bearing **L** through a gateway. The track climbs slightly then continues to a junction with a metalled road. Turn **R** in the direction of Witherslack Hall. Turn **L** at the hall along a track signed to Knott Wood.

5 Follow the track, immediately bearing **L** and ignoring the bridleway to the right. A quick descent leads to a field by some cottages. Bear **R**, away from the cottages, to a gate on the opposite side of the field. Pass through the gate and continue along the track with the wall on your left. The track then breaks out into open country and leads to a junction. Turn **R**, signposted with a blue bridleway waymarker, and bear **L** at the fork to climb to a gate in the wall.

6 From the gate, follow singletrack into the wood. The next section is one of the highlights of the route as it soon starts to descend. Turn **L** by a cairn just after a steep section of descent and continue down to the road. Turn **R**. Follow the road for 2km **ignoring** roads on the left. At a sharp left-hand bend turn **R** through a gate onto a track, signed *Bridleway, Witherslack Hall.* Climb to the hall, turning **L** through a gateway at the very top of the hill.

7 At the road, turn **L** and follow the minor road **SA** for approximately 3km, passing two roads on the left.

8 After a left-hand bend, the road begins to climb. On the brow of the hill, turn **R** onto a track by an old kiln. Climb steeply towards a gate, following the track to the right at the gate. At the T-junction at the top of the hill, turn **L** and follow the bridleway through two gates onto a fast descent to Row. Join tarmac (**with care** – this is a residential area and there could be vehicles manoeuvring) and continue **SA** down to the A5074.

9 Turn **R** and continue for 300m. At a sharp left-hand bend, turn **R** onto a lane and climb through the village of Howe. Descend to a crossroads and turn **R** towards Flodder Hall. After 1.5km, rejoin the A5074 and turn **R** towards Gilpin Bridge.

10 At the T-junction turn **R** past the Gilpin Bridge Pub (or stop off for a swift pint may be?) then take the cycleway back to the old A590 and car.

Making a day of it

The **Cartmel Fell** ride *(page 19)* lies to the east of this route. Linking the two would create a long, but technically straightforward day out.

ABOVE TROUTBECK

Troutbeck & Jenkin Crag

20km

Introduction

Set in the hotspot of Ambleside and the surrounding area, this is a varied and surprisingly technical ride that is great for an evening or when there are other things that must be done during the day, and makes an exciting night ride for the more adventurous. It's also a nice way of getting out from Ambleside over towards Kentmere, High Street and Garburn, if you're looking for a longer day out.

The Ride

Although the route starts with the often busy A591, a bit of road work acts as a nice warm-up as the start of the off-road terrain starts steeply. Some great little downhills lead to Town End before tarmac climbs gently to Dubbs Road. More gradual climbing leads past Dubbs Reservoir and toward the top of the speedy downhill that takes you down into Limefitt Park. Climb back up to Troutbeck and then Robin Lane for the final downhill. This can be very testing depending on whether or not you decide on the escape route or commit yourself to the rocky steps. Either way, this is one of the better downhills in the area.

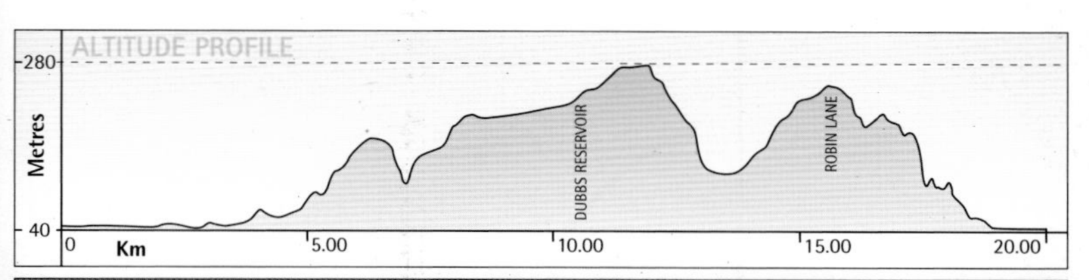

TROUTBECK & JENKIN CRAG — **GRADE: ▲**

DISTANCE: 20KM

START/FINISH: BROW HEAD FARM

PARKING: AMBLESIDE, OR FREE PARKING AT BROW HEAD FARM

PUBLIC HOUSE: MANY CHOICES IN AMBLESIDE

TOTAL ASCENT: 967M

GRID REFERENCE: NY 370 045

CAFÉ: AMBLESIDE

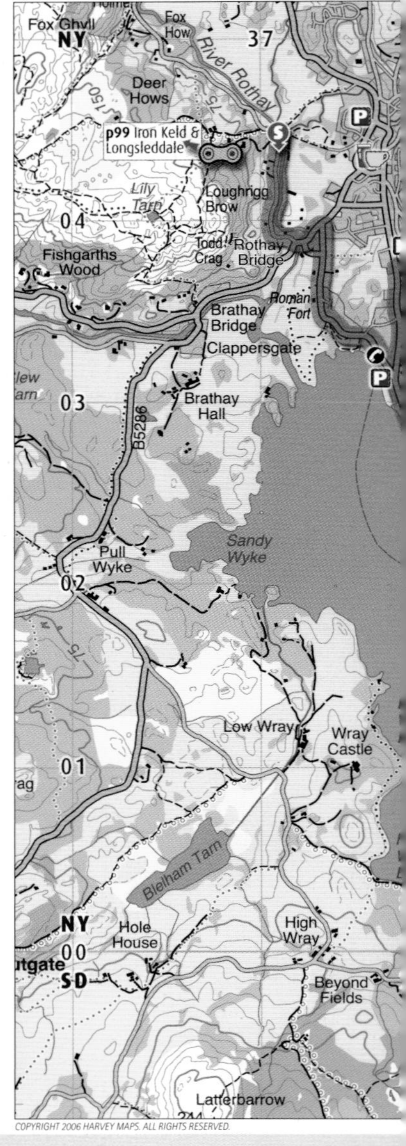

Fox Ghyll
NY
Fox How
37
River Rothay
Deer Hows
150
75
p99 Iron Keld & Longsleddale
Lily Tarn
Loughrigg Brow
04
Todd Crag
Rothay Bridge
Fishgarths Wood
Roman Fort
Brathay Bridge
Clappersgate
03
B5286
Brathay Hall
Sandy Wyke
Pull Wyke
02
Low Wray
Wray Castle
01
Blelham Tarn
NY
00
SD
Hole House
High Wray
Beyond Fields
Latterbarrow

Troutbeck & Jenkin Crag

Directions – Troutbeck & Jenkin Crag

S From the car park head south to Rothay Bridge. Turn **L** and follow the one-way system, turning **R** to Waterhead. At Waterhead turn **R** onto the A591 following signs for Windermere and Kendal. Be careful as the road is narrow in parts and for some reason the cars seem to ignore cyclists. After 4.5km turn **L** onto Mirk Lane opposite Ecclerigg Church (shortly after signs for the Brockhole Centre on your right and the Merewood Hotel on your left).

2 Climb steeply past buildings and through woods to a road. Turn **L**. After a short distance, more track takes you steeply uphill once again.

3 At the T-junction with the road, turn **R** for 700m, passing a track (bridleway) which doubles back on the right and then a bridleway on the left. Soon after a layby on the right, turn **R** onto a bridleway and descend towards Town End. Cross the road, heading **SA** onto a signed bridleway and descend to two footbridges (or ford the river). Head up the grass bank to the road.

4 Turn **R** and then first **L** onto Moorhowe Road, climbing steeply at first. After 2km, on a right-hand bend, turn **L** along a track with a dead end sign. This is Dubbs Road.

5 Head north, climbing pleasantly past Dubbs Reservoir and through gates for 2.5km to a T-junction with the Garburn Road. Turn **L**, downhill, almost back on yourself, heading south-west. A great downhill follows. Don't get too carried away – turn **R** onto a bridleway after 600m, doubling back on yourself and passing through a gate.

6 Continue downhill, taking the next **L** (alongside the wall) and dropping through a final gate into the caravan park. Follow bridleway signs along the road through the centre of the park and join the main road.

7 Turn **L** and, after 200m, turn **R** onto a track just before the church, by an old water trough. Climb gently up singletrack, keeping **L** at the bridleway junction, to join the road.

8 Turn **L** and, after a short distance, turn **R** up the road past the Post Office. Climb steeply for a short distance on tarmac and continue for 1.2km to a fork, **ignoring** bridleways on the left. Bear **L** (signed *Jenkin Crag*), through two gates. After the second, keep **R**, uphill, to High Skelghyll Farm. Dismount and walk through the farm buildings, then saddle-up for the next descent.

9 The final section past Jenkin Crag and through Skelghyll Woods is a joy. Some steep rocky sections need some commitment, as do the root-covered boulders. This is a popular walk so take care. The final steep tarmac brings you out behind the mountain rescue centre on the outskirts of Ambleside. All you need to do is find you car, a café or a pub.

Making a day of it

This route makes an excellent start to several longer routes for those based in Ambleside. Link to the **Garburn Pass** *(page 25)*, then to the **Longsleddale** route *(page 69)* and, from there, as far as you like!

Ings & Winster

23km

Introduction

A surprising good low-level ride on the outskirts of Staveley. If you prefer country lanes and bridleways to rocky slopes, then this is the route for you. Generally, the lanes you will encounter are only used by local traffic and are very quiet. There is very little technical off-road, although there is a short steep section just after Thornyfields and a great downhill after Birk Moss. A great introduction to 'proper' Lake District mountain biking if you've just come off the family trails at Grizedale and want a longer ride.

The Ride

From Ings, the route heads south-west to Borwick Fold before going off-road for a short section and back onto country lanes to Crook. Then it heads south-east, taking you through an extended off-road section past Crook Hall and along trails past High House and Birk Moss. It then takes you through to Winster via the pretty hamlet of Thornyfields. From here you climb north-east on country lanes, before a great trail leads to Lindeth Lane. This takes you onto the B5284, the only busy road, which has one short climb past the Windermere Golf Club before heading off north-east on country lanes back to Ings.

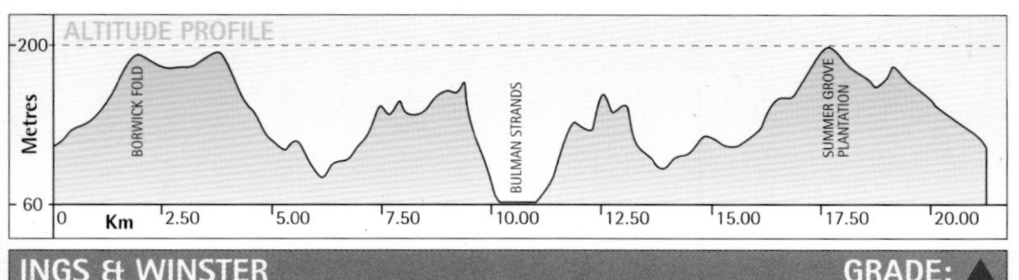

INGS & WINSTER **GRADE: ▲**

DISTANCE: 23KM

TOTAL ASCENT: 670M

START/FINISH: INGS

GRID REFERENCE: SD 444 987

PARKING: LIMITED AT INGS, PARTICULARLY AT WEEKENDS

CAFÉ: WILF'S Tel: 01539 822 329

PUBLIC HOUSE: WATERMILL INN, INGS Tel: 01539 821 309

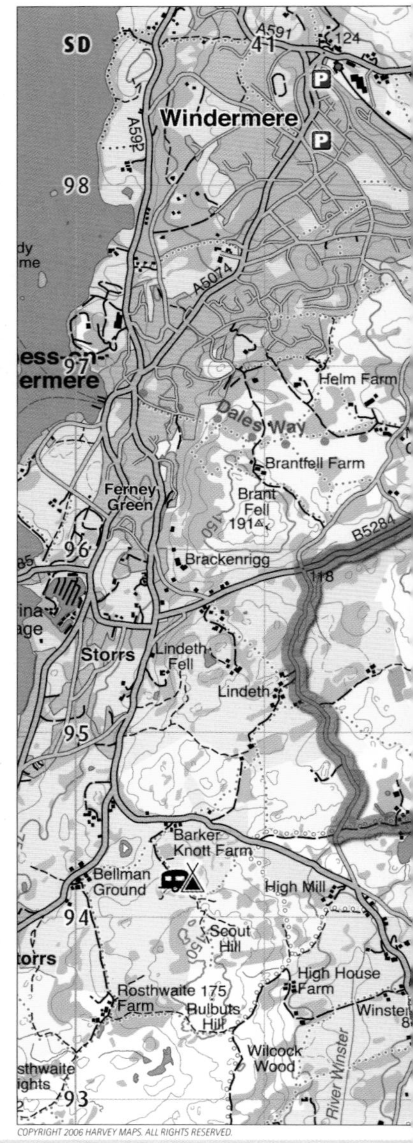
SD
A591
41
124
Windermere
A592
98
A5074
97
Helm Farm
Dales Way
Brantfell Farm
Ferney Green
Brant Fell
191
B5284
96
Brackenrigg
118
Storrs
Lindeth Fell
Lindeth
95
Barker Knott Farm
Bellman Ground
High Mill
94
Scout Hill
High House Farm
Rosthwaite 175 Farm
Bulbuts Hill
Winster
Wilcock Wood
River Winster
93

Ings & Winster

Directions – Ings & Winster

S Go **SA** up the small lane, signed ***Borwick Fold***, opposite the small car park and pub in Ings. Follow this for 2km, gradually climbing to a T-junction.

2 Turn **R** and, after 200m, turn **L** onto a bridleway towards Borwick Fold. Follow the bridleway, which is vague in places, south through a field. After 500m, join the Dales Way and turn **L** along it to emerge on a country lane. Turn **R** along this, heading south-east and downhill for 2.25km to the village of Crook.

3 At the busy T-junction turn **R**, and take the first **L** onto Dobby Lane shortly afterwards. Climb to a T-junction and turn **L**. After 300m, turn **R** onto a small lane signed *Crook Hall*. At the fork, bear **R** (still signed Crook Hall) and, at a second fork by a cattle grid, go **SA** over the cattle grid and through a gate on the **L**.

4 Follow the wall and trail west north-west to a T- junction with a pathway. Turn **L** and head south-west on poorly defined trails to a bridge, and then uphill to join a confluence of several routes. **Ignoring** footpaths, bear **L** then **R** (marked with bridleway sign) and follow the trail for 500m to the buildings at Birk Moss. **Do not** go through the farmyard, but take the bridleway to the **L** of the buildings. Climb to a T-junction, turn **L** and head south. A great little descent, initially on a trail then vaguely across fields, leads to a junction with the Crosthwaite road.

5 Turn **R** and, after 500m, take the bridleway on the **L** that passes in front of Crook Foot, initially following the picturesque stream north west before heading to Thornyfields. Bear **L** in front of the houses and then turn **L** behind the barn and through a gate with a bridleway sign. A short, sharp climb follows and as we know, many ascents are followed by descents. This one takes you down to the A5074.

6 Turn **R**, heading towards Winster and take the first turning on the **R** in front of the pub. (Of course you could always stop for refreshments!) Follow this uphill for 1km until it flattens out and passes Knipe Tarn. Shortly after the tarn, pass a turning on the right and start to descend – but don't go too fast because you need to turn **L** up an unsigned trail 500m after the tarn.

7 Follow this west for 1.6km, **ignoring** turnings, with a good downhill finish bringing you to Lindeth Lane. Turn sharp **R** and head north for 1.6km to a crossroads with the B5284. Turn **R** uphill (carefully – it can be fast and busy) for 1.5km, passing Windermere Golf Club and take the second lane on the **L** after the club (after a small tarn), heading north-east towards Borwick Fold for 2km to a T-junction.

8 Turn **L** and ride past the entrance to Yews to a T-junction. (The bridleway through Yews shown on some maps is actually a footpath, so **don't take it**) Turn **R** to Whasdike and turn **R** onto a bridleway in front of the building. Go through a gate into a copse and continue **SA** (a footpath goes off left) on a great little bit of singletrack. Leave the copse via another gate and bear **L** round a hilly knoll to the lane that leads back to Ings. Turn **L** and retrace your route to the car.

Making a day of it

Ride north to **Garburn Pass** *(page 25)* to create a long a fairly technical route, or south to search out some more gentle bridleways and go exploring.

ABOVE DUNNERDALE

Broughton Moor & Seathwaite

21km

Introduction

This is a great day out. Even though the ride is only 21km in length, it feels bigger and takes a bit longer than you would think. It packs in everything for the experienced rider: good singletrack, technical climbs and storming descents.

Route finding can be a little tricky at times, as tracks can be vague or unmarked – or there can simply be a fair few to choose from – so a compass is always useful to make sure you're heading in the right direction!

The Ride

The ride starts in the forest of Broughton Moor, initially heading east on forest roads before some great singletrack bridleways lead to Stephenson Ground. From the farm, head north-west along Long Mire (not as bad as it sounds) before a storming downhill drops into Seathwaite and the Newfield Inn. A bit of tarmac spinning leads down the Dunnerdale Valley – a beautiful area, not visited by so many tourists, where a pleasant track takes you through some great countryside and Birks Forest, to come out at Birks. Push uphill for a short while before heading east, back over the Dunnerdale Fells and round Ravens Crag to what looks like a fierce uphill, but is actually very rideable. Downhills and singletrack take you back to Stephenson Ground and the start.

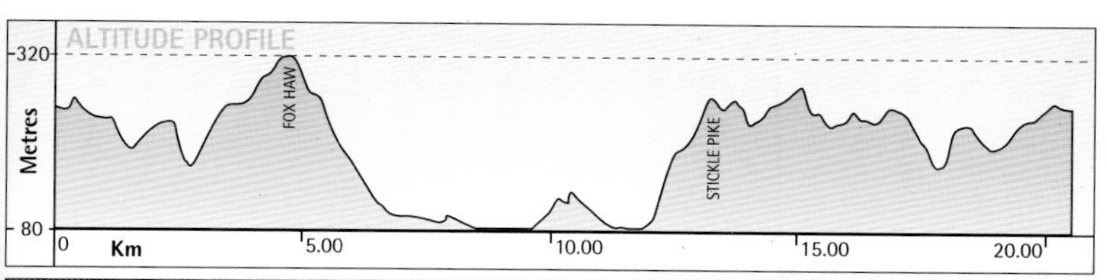

BROUGHTON MOOR & SEATHWAITE **GRADE: ▲**

DISTANCE: 21KM
TOTAL ASCENT: 818M
START/FINISH: BROUGHTON FOREST
GRID REFERENCE: SD 253 927
PARKING: BROUGHTON FOREST CAR PARK
CAFÉ: BLUEBIRD CAFÉ – CONISTON Tel: 01539 441 649
PUBLIC HOUSE: IN CONISTON OR NEWFIELD INN, SEATHWAITE Tel: 01229 716 208

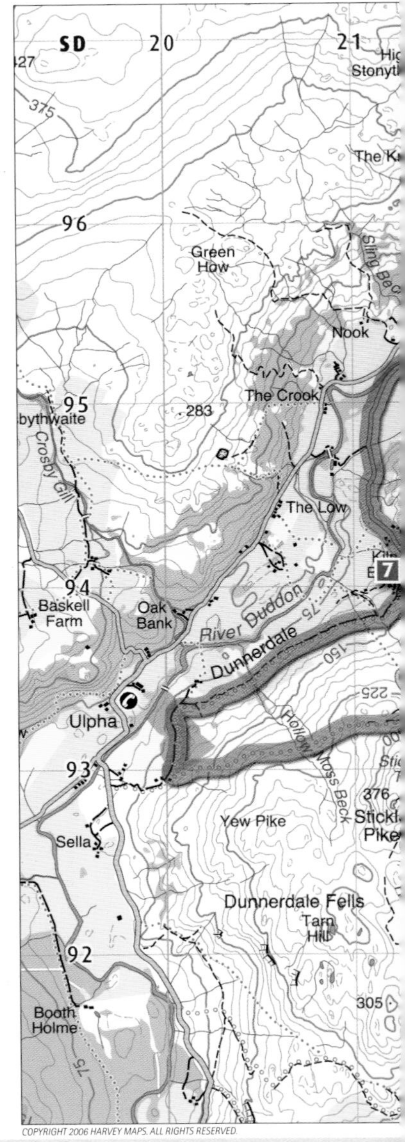
SD
20
21
427
375
High Stonyt
The K
96
Green How
Sling Bec
Nook
95
bythwaite
Crosby Gill
283
The Crook
The Low
94
Baskell Farm
Oak Bank
River Duddon
75
Dunnerdale
150
225
Ulpha
Hollow Moss Beck
93
Sella
Yew Pike
376
Stickl Pike
Dunnerdale Fells
Tarn Hill
92
305
Booth Holme
7

Broughton Moor & Seathwaite

Directions – Broughton Moor & Seathwaite

S From the car park, head downhill (north-east) along the road for 500m and turn **L** through a gate into the forest. Descend on forest road to a right-hand bend and start to climb.

2 **Ignore** the forest road on the left. On the brow of the climb, turn **L** onto a bridleway to descend on superb singletrack. At the junction with the forest road below, turn **L**.

3 The fire road descends to cross a concrete bridge and climb steeply to another fire road. Turn **L** and then **R (easy to miss)** onto singletrack just after a right-hand bend. Follow this orgasmic singletrack to drop steeply to yet another fire road. Turn **R** then immediately **L** down a bridleway. Continue through the gate to the lane and turn **R**, crossing the bridge and climbing steeply to the farm (Stephenson Ground).

4 At the farm, turn **R** through a gate, signed bridleway and then bear **L** heading towards Seathwaite (the bridleway right leads to Walna Scar). Head north-west, climbing steeply alongside the wall and follow the bridleway across the stream. Follow the track between walls by the stream, passing through a second gated wall to a 3-way junction.

5 Turn **L** and continue downhill by the wall. As the wall bears left, bear **R** at the fork (essentially **SA**). Pleasant singletrack leads through undulating terrain (trending uphill), eventually opening out and reaching two cairns. **Ignore** the track to the right and continue **SA** onto a technical and fast (or as fast as you want to make it) descent to Seathwaite and the Newfield Inn – of course it could end sooner if you come off!

6 Turn **L** along the road, following the River Duddon to the west and then south. Bear **L** at the road junction just before Hall Bridge (phone box) heading in the direction of Broughton Mills. As the road bears sharply left and uphill, turn **R** onto a bridleway running through Far Kiln Bank.

7 Follow the pleasant track through Birks Wood to Low Birks, turning **L** up a steep bridleway opposite the house. As the bridleway becomes vague, keep heading **SA** and east over the Dunnerdale Fells. The track can be difficult to find but offers some great singletrack. Contour around the side of the hill to the road.

Note: The bridleway can be difficult to find. If you hit the road near the cattle grid, you are too far north – turn **R** and head uphill to the top of the hill and turn **L** (east) onto a signed bridleway.

8 If you managed to keep to the bridleway, you will arrive at the road at the top of the hill. Go **SA** (east) onto the signed bridleway. Follow the bridleway downhill to a crossroads with a larger track. Continue **SA** over this onto a sometimes boggy bridleway leading to a wall and then contouring around the hillside (this is Raven Crag).

9 Follow this bridleway up the challenging climb to the crest of the ridge to meet another bridleway coming from Stainton Ground. Turn **L** and descend, following the bridleway to Jackson Ground. **Do not** go into the farm – follow the track around it to join a bridleway heading south-east and back to Stephenson Ground. From here, retrace your steps to your car or follow the optional fire road route.

As you join the main forestry road, head south downhill, bearing **L** at the first junction and following the track for some way. Bear **R** at the next junction, cross a bridge and descend to a fork. Bear **L**, turn **L** again at the next junction and follow the track back to the start.

Making a day of it

Adding the **Walna Scar** ride *(page 161)* to this would create a nice figure-8 ride.

STEVE HEADING & AL SHELDON ON THE SLATE

Iron Keld, Hodge Close & Loughrigg 24km

Introduction

This is a great ride into the heart of the south Lakes, travelling among some great mountain scenery without having to gain a lot of height! Navigation is straightforward, as the route follows well waymarked bridleways at all times. In addition, the bridleways are mostly stone-based, so this is a route that can be ridden year-round. There are plenty of opportunities for café/pub stops along the way.

The Ride

Head north from Grizedale Forest in the direction of Tarn Hows to the rocky Tarn Hows byway, which leads over to the busy Coniston/Ambleside road. More tracks lead straight up past Hodge Close Quarry and into Little Langdale via a tricky climb and long rocky descent. Climb up the hill for a fast, and again rocky descent into the picturesque village of Elterwater in Great Langdale Valley and take the road to climb over to Loughrigg for a fun descent down the scenic terrace. (Watch out for walkers here.) Climb back over Loughrigg and hit the road out of Skelwith Bridge to the bridleway to Iron Keld, a National Trust owned forest which has been dramatically altered recently due to harvesting. A rocky but fast descent leads us to rejoin the Tarn Hows byway for the return stretch to the car park at High Cross.

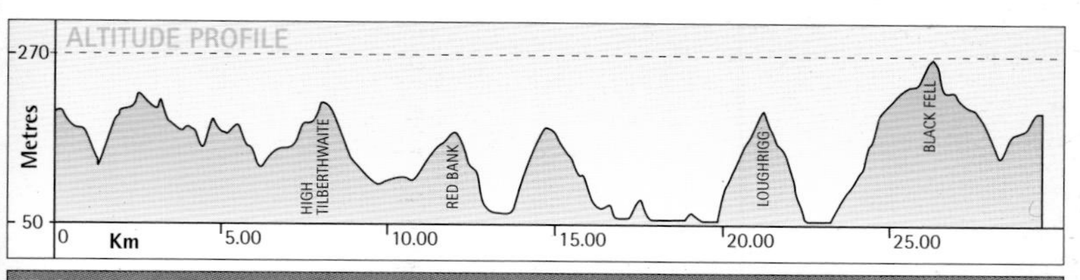

IRON KELD, HODGE CLOSE & LOUGHRIGG **GRADE: ▲**

DISTANCE: 24KM **TOTAL ASCENT:** 885M

START/FINISH: HIGH CROSS (HAWKSHEAD HILL) CAR PARK IN GRIZEDALE FOREST

GRID REFERENCE: SD 332986 **PARKING:** FREE CAR PARK

CAFÉ: HAWKSHEAD OR CONISTON **PUBLIC HOUSE:** HAWKSHEAD OR CONISTON

Great Langdale
NY
30
31
Great Langdale Beck
06
Langdale Boulder
362
Side Pike
Oakhowe Crag
Lingmoor Tarn
Hag Wood
383
Upper Spout Crag
05
Bleatarn House
Blea Tarn
470
Brown How
Lingmoor Fell
04
Busk Pike
Hollin Crag
Castle Howe
Little Langdale Tarn
6
03
River Brathay
Greenburn Beck
Runestone Quarry
405
Mine (disused)
02
Birk Fell
528
Blake Rigg
High Tilberthwaite
5
01
Tilberthwaite Quarry
Mines (disused)
NY
Red Gill Head
Wether
00
SD
Crook Beck
Yewdale Fells
White Gill
Mines (disused)
Yewdale Crag
99
The Blue Quarries (disused)
Mart Crag
Yew Pike
Rigg Head
Far End
Stone
A593

Iron Keld, Hodge Close & Loughrigg
p183 Big Day Out
p81 Troutbeck & Jenkin Cragg
Silver Howe
The Lea
Grasmere
Dale End
White Moss
Rydal Water
Heron Island
Rydal Mount
Rydal Hall
Rydal
Rydal Park
Pelter Bridge
Rydal Cave
Rough Intake
Lanty Scar
Raven Crag
Red Bank
Loughrigg Fell
Intake Wood
Chapel Stile
Elterwater
Low Wood
Loughrigg Holme
Fox Ghyll
Fox How
River Rothay
Deer Hows
Low Sweden Bridge
Ambleside
Cumbria Way
Nab Island
Elter Water
Oaks
Loughrigg Tarn
Tarn Foot
Lily Tarn
Loughrigg Brow
Fletcher's Wood
Fishgarths Wood
Todd Crag
Rothay Bridge
Roman Fort
Hacket
Skelwith Force
Skelwith Bridge
River Brathay
Brathay Bridge
Clappersgate
Colwith Force
Park How
Skelwith Fold
Slew Tarn
Brathay Hall
High Park
Great How
Park Fell
Holmes Head Farm
Pull Wyke
Sandy Wyke
High Oxen Fell
Black Fell
Drunken Duck
Low Wray
Wray Castle
Low Wray Bay
High Crag
Yew Tree Tarn
Tom Heights
Sunny Brow
Blelham Tarn
High Wray Bay
Tarn Hows
Field Head House
Hole House
High Wray
Outgate
Beyond Fields
Knipe Fold
Belmount
Tarn Hows Hotel
Sandy Ground
Latterbarrow
Thurs Gill
Hawkshead Hill
B5285
Keen Ground
Black Beck
Ferry Summer only

Directions – Iron Keld, Hodge Close & Loughrigg

S Exit the car park **SA** over the main road onto the minor road opposite, heading for Tarn Hows. After 1.5km, drop sharply downhill and turn **L** onto a wide byway immediately after a road junction on the right. Pass behind the cottage (Borwick Lodge is signposted on the right).

2 Follow the byway for approximately 2.8km, **ignoring** all turnings, to join a metalled track, follow it down to the main Coniston/Ambleside road. Continue **SA** up the singletrack lane opposite.

3 Climb steeply and then descend to the farm at High Oxen Fell. Go **SA** through a gate onto a bridleway as tarmac ends. Climb to another gate and then descend to a third at Hodge Close. Please ensure they are all closed behind you.

4 At the T-junction with a metalled lane, turn **L** and descend around corners through buildings. Directly opposite the last cottage on the left, turn **R** onto a track through a gate. Descend to a long right-hand bend, turning **L** to descend a rocky (slate) track in a gully immediately beyond the bend (**ignoring** the first track on the left, which stays high). Drop into the woods, cross a stream and climb a short hill, to a T-junction. Turn **L**, continuing **SA** as the track levels out.

5 Keep going to High Tilberthwaite Farm. At the farm, continue into the farmyard and turn sharp **R** through a gate. Please walk whilst in the yard. Follow the rocky track for 1.5km over some quite challenging terrain with ever-improving views of the mountains. After descending to a second gate, continue **SA**, **ignoring** the track coming in from the right. Drop to a metalled road and then to a T-junction with the road which is at the foot of Wrynose Pass.

6 Turn **R**, following the lane for 1km, continuing **SA** at the junction and climbing to the top of the hill. Turn **L** up a narrow lane to Dale End Farm. The road gives way to track as it passes the farm and descends to a gate. Continue **SA** past the gate (**ignore** the track to the left), join tarmac and descend to a T-junction. Turn **L** to Elterwater.

7 Immediately beyond the green in Elterwater, fork **L** (between the pub and the post office) and ride to a crossroads at the main road. Go **SA** onto the lane opposite to start the climb to Loughrigg. After 500m, turn **R** at the T-junction and continue to climb. The pain is only short-lived and you soon reach a T-junction.

Optional Route

Turn **R** to descend towards Loughrigg Tarn. Unfortunately there's no legal right of way for MTBs around the tarn, so stick to the road. Take the second road on the **R** (after 1.7km), passing the tarn on your left and drop down a very steep hill to Skelwith Bridge. **Take great care**, this road really is steep and narrow. Watch out for cars and keep your speed down!

8 At the T-junction turn **L**, quickly turning **R** onto a bridleway by a sign on the wall for Rydal. Follow this scenic trail (avoiding walkers where possible). It is not technical but can be narrow in places, so please be courteous to other users. Arriving at the shore of Rydal Water, (a great place for a swim on a hot day), the bridleway sinks beneath the water. Look for the obvious rock step – the shoreline is shallow enough to cycle through and good fun for onlookers when you hit submerged boulders! Alternatively, MTBs are now allowed to take the high route via the caves (less wet). Continue along the obvious route to Pelter Bridge. **Don't** go over the bridge, but turn **R** along the road.

9 Turn **R** onto a bridleway after 1.5km. Climb to Brow Head Farm and follow the obvious track **SA** as it heads south-west and downhill to skirt Ivy Crag. Ignore the bridleway to the right and follow singletrack to a gate.

10 Turn **R** at the fork beyond the gate to a T-junction with the road, beside a postbox in a wall. Turn **R**, then immediately **L** and descend steeply to join the main road at Skelwith Bridge.

11 Go **SA** over the road junction onto the A593 towards Coniston. Climb for 1.2km until the road starts to descend and turn **L** onto a signed bridleway.

12 Tricky climbing with fantastic views all around. After 1km go through a gap in the wall, with the buildings of Low Arnside just ahead. Turn immediately **L** (and uphill), following bridleway signs. The rewarding downhill comes 800m later through a gate into Iron Keld plantation. (**Ignore** the track off to the left at the gate.) Descend to the gate which opens onto your earlier route.

13 Turn **L** and retrace your steps to the road. Turn **R**, climb Hawkshead Hill and follow the road to the car park at High Cross.

THE TWISTING DESCENT INTO BOOT

Miterdale – Eskdale

26km

Introduction

Whilst all other areas of the Lakes will be jam packed with tourists, walkers and fellow mountain bikers, this is an area where you will find solitude, "far from the madding crowd". On a clear day there are fabulous views across Burnmoor Tarn and Eskdale Fell, with the Scafell range beyond. This ride offers everything for the enthusiastic mountain biker, forest bridleways, grinding uphills on good tracks, great singletrack and storming descents – it really is one of the better rides in the area. The route gains little height but the open fells can be very exposed to the wind, the paths can be vague and, after rain, certain areas can be boggy. Navigation skills would be useful if you don't know the area.

The Ride

Starting at the bottom of Hardknott Pass – which is said to be the steepest road in the UK – an easy bridleway follows the River Esk on its south bank. After a short road section past Eskdale Outward Bound Centre, head north-east up the Miterdale valley. A scenic trail through woodland on good bridleways leads to the climb from Bakestead, where poor trails through the wood lead to a great ascent onto Tongue Moor and over to Burnmoor Tarn. Join the old 'Coffin Road', an old road along which the dead were taken from Wasdale to be buried at the church in Boot. Pass Burnmoor Tarn on open fell, which eventually becomes a superb technical singletrack descent into the village of Boot. Follow the road back to the start, stopping at the Woolpack Inn for some light refreshment.

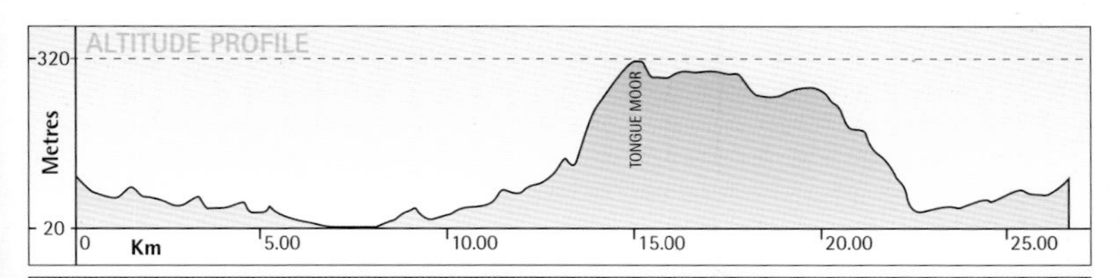

MITERDALE – ESKDALE **GRADE: ▲**

DISTANCE: 26KM

START/FINISH: START OF HARDKNOTT PASS

PARKING: LAYBY AT THE START OF HARDKNOTT PASS

PUBLIC HOUSE: WOOLPACK INN, ESKDALE Tel: 01946 723 230

TOTAL ASCENT: 723M

GRID REFERENCE: NY 212 011

CAFÉ: SEVERAL IN CONISTON

Buckbarrow
Broad Crag
Bull Crag
NY
13
14
15
16
Wast Water
Greendale
Harrow Head
Buckbarrow
Tosh Tarn
Cinderdale Beck
05
Ashness How
Wasdale Hall
Woodhow Tarn
Woodhow
Nether Wasdale
04
Lund Bridge
The Screes
Low Adam Crag
Illgill Head
477
Flass
Easthwaite
Pens End Crag
536
Whin Rigg
Greathall Gill
Great Grain Gill
Little Grain Gill
Robin Gill
03
Latterbarrow
201
394
02
Great Bank
Low Place
White Moss
River Mite
Aln House
229
Bleatarn Hill
Siney Tarn
Blea Tarn
01
Fell End
Hollinghead Crag
Bell Stand
Beckfoot Station
Plumgarth
Beckfoot Quarry
Eskdale Green
Outward Bound School
Dalegarth Hall
NY
00
SD
Irton Road
39
Hollowstones
The Green
High Frith
Milkingstead Wood
Silver Knott
Bankend Wood
Forge Bridge
Rigg
Redbrow Bank
177
Muncaster
1
2
3
4
5

Miterdale – Eskdale
Slight Side
Great How
Burnmoor Tarn
Eskdale
Boot
Stony Tarn
Eel Tarn
Dawsonground Crags
Great Barrow
Peelplace Noddle
Brotherilkeld
Jubilee Bridge
Hardknott Castle (MEDIOBOGDVM)
Doctor's Br.
Penny Hill Farm
Low Birker
Wha House Farm
Whahouse Bridge
Birker Fell
Taw House
Terrace Route
Hare Crag
Goat Crag
Raven Crag
Broad Tongue
Quagrigg Moss
Horn Crag
Sampson's Stones
Silvery Bleld Crag
High Scarth Crag
Round Scar
Brock Crag
Yew Crags
Demming Crag
Kepple Crag
Gate Crag
Hartley Crag
Low Birker Tarn
Birker Force
Armont House
Esk View Farm
Boat How
Whillan Beck
Brookshaw Beck
Cowcove Beck
Catcove Beck
River Esk
Hardknott Gill

Directions – Miterdale – Eskdale

S From the layby, head downhill on the road for 1km. Just before Whahouse Bridge, turn **L** onto a bridleway and follow this along the left bank of the River Esk. Please walk through the yard at Penny Hill Farm.

2 Just beyond Penny Hill Farm, turn **L** immediately before Doctor's Bridge to follow the bridleway to Low Birker. Pleasant riding leads to the road. Turn **R**, and then **L** by The Green pub.

3 Follow the road past the Outward Bound Centre and through Eskdale Green (stopping for any supplies at the post office). Turn **R** just beyond a left-hand turn to the train station and by a school sign onto what looks like a private drive. Follow it past the school. The road turns to track and crosses a bridge. Bear **R** on good trails, following a bridleway to the farm at Low Place.

4 Continue on the left-hand bank of the river to Miterdale Head, where the bridleway can be seen going through a large gap made by the two forests. Follow the poor bridleway steeply uphill.

5 The bridleway is vague to non-existent in places. Keep heading roughly **SA** and north east, aiming for gates through walls. As you reach the highest point on Tongue Moor, the fells are laid out before you, with Burnmoor Tarn centre stage. Follow some great singletrack to the eventual confluence of paths from Illgill Head and the 'Coffin Road' from Wasdale.

Note: There are often paths better than the bridleway that lead to this intersection, so you may find yourself higher up the fell than expected. In clear conditions you can see the 'Coffin Road' and correct your mistake. In bad weather, keep your map and compass handy.

6 Turn **R** along the bridleway heading for Burnmoor Tarn. The track skirts around the edge of the tarn - good for cooling the feet on hotter days - and then over Bulatt Bridge. A little further on the path divides. Continue **SA** along the bridleway (a footpath bears right to Burnmoor Lodge while another bears left to a footbridge in the distance).

7 The trail is now a bit lumpy bumpy until it passes an old ruin on the right at Eller How and turns to decidedly technical downhill singletrack, which is an absolute joy. Part way down the track you have a choice of two gates, turn **R** (signed *Boot* in faded paint on the wall) and continue to Boot.

8 At the main road, turn **L** and follow the road to your car. If you have a little energy left, you can always test yourself on the road going over Hardknott Pass!

Making a day of it

Keep riding north from the top of this ride to Wasdale Head and there are bridleways running over the Styhead and Black Sail passes. Proper 'old school' mountain biking (i.e. involving carrying!), they'll turn the day into a long one...

top 10 Singletracks

Lakeland singletrack vary from the wooded to the moorland and then to the man-made. Some are swoopy, some are tricky – they're all fun. Check out these suggestions for our pick of the best.

1 **Hazel Seat to Low Dale Park** **(Grizedale & Esthwaite)** **GR SD 368 924 – 350 918**
2.5km of woodland singletrack, starting with a wide and steep climb before narrowing at the summit. Fantastic steep singletrack descent out of the forest onto open land.

2 **Martindale** **(Ullswater Singletrack)** **GR NY 416 156 – 434 165**
Perfect white singletrack over the top of the ridge leads to a fast grassy descent into Martindale.

3 **Broughton Moor** **(Broughton Moor & Seathwaite)** **GR SD 246 928 – 238 929**
Short and sweet with a fast descent, this will have you wishing for more!

4 **Appletree Holme to Climb Stile** **(Blawith Loop)** **GR SD 277 888 – 258 908**
3.6km of superb Lakeland singletrack across open fell. It doesn't get much better than this!

5 **Carter Ground to Stephenson Ground** **(Broughton Moor & Seathwaite)** **GR SD 214 933 – 235 932**
Classic Lakeland singletrack across open fell. A distance of 3.8km.

Witherslack Hall to Minor Road **(Whitbarrow Scar)** **GR SD 435 859 – 435 835**

Ok, so it's not all singletrack, but once you're in the trees you won't care a bit! Very fast in summer, watch out for horses and limestone when it's wet. Distance is 2k.

Ullswater **(Ullswater Singletrack)** **GR NY 424 196 – 400 161**

Not all that narrow, not at all swoopy and can be busy. Why's it included? Because it's technical as anything, right on the edge of what's rideable (for the average rider) and is fun. Awesome!

Lonscale Fell **(Two short rides from Keswick)** **GR NY 292 280 – 293 261**

Fast narrow bits, technical climbs, slippery rock (in the wet) and a massive drop to one side.

Mosedale **(Skiddaw)** **GR NY 287 291 – 313 314**

Fast, rutted, rocky, grassy, sketchy... and it goes on for ages.

The North Face Trail **(in Grizedale Forest)** **GR SD 337 944**

The first purpose built trail in Cumbria. A mix of singletrack, fire road and wooden obstacles. No walkers to worry about either!

SECTION 3

Enduros

Now we're talking. Pack your sarnies and your chain lube. These are big, tough rides (for big, tough riders?) that'll probably take you all day. They're challenging routes for fit and experienced mountain bikers – you know – proper riding. Riding where you might describe the route as 'a bit of a beast'.

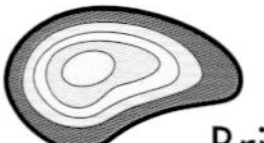

Enduros **route finder**

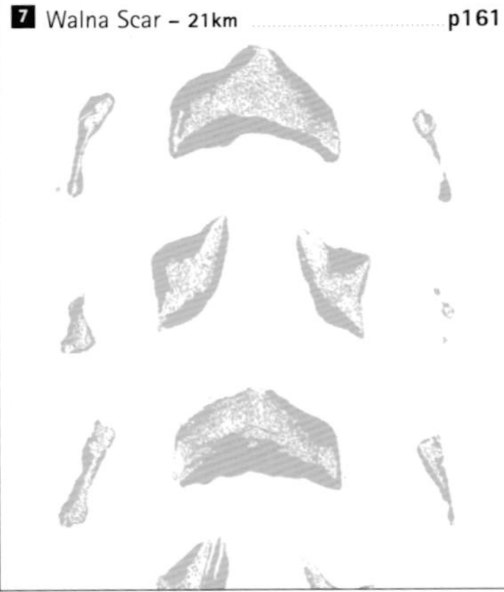

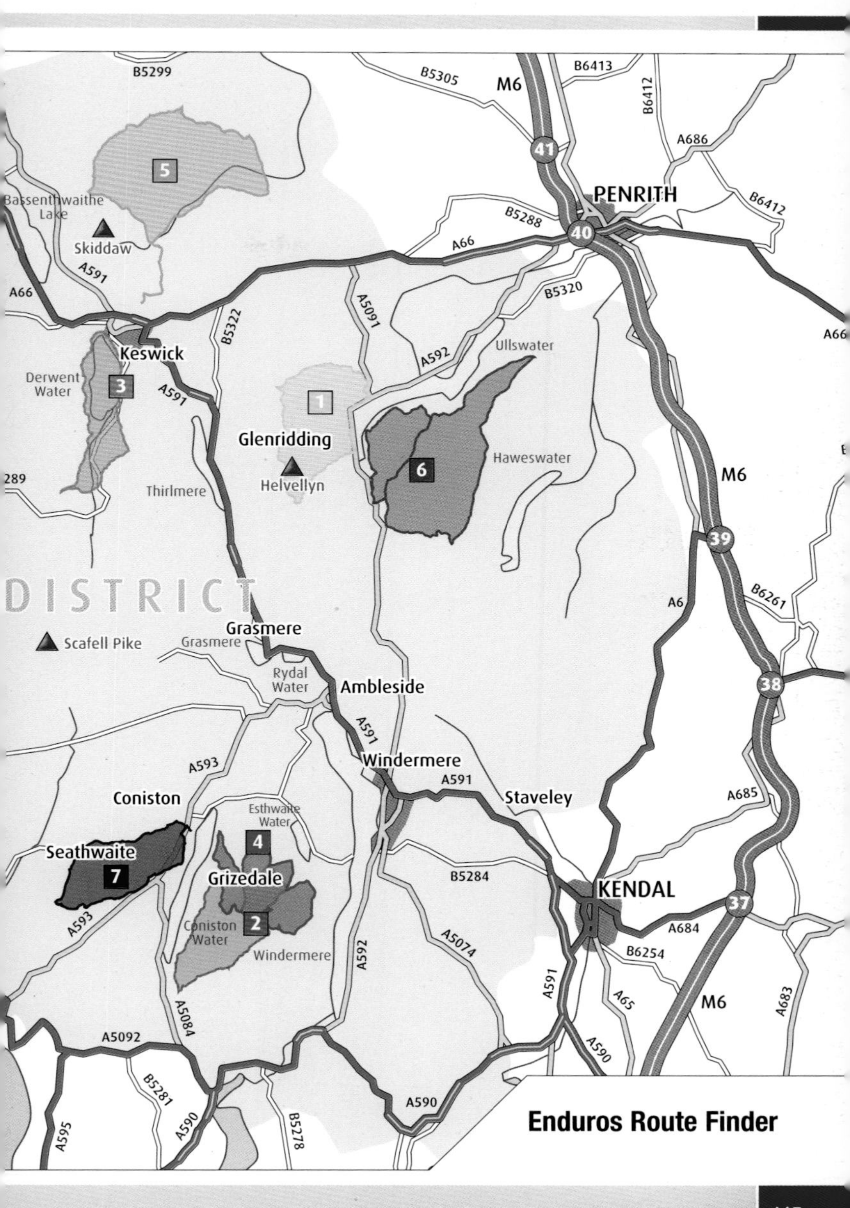

Enduros Route Finder

FINISHING OFF STICKS PASS

Helvellyn

22.5km

Introduction

Helvellyn is the highest mountain in England that you can legally ride on a bike. (Whether or not you do actually ride is down to you!) So be prepared for lots of climbing, big views and a huge descent. This route gives you a choice of three descents: a relatively easy track, a mainly-singletrack-with-a-couple-of-steep-bits option and a ridiculously rocky decent that'll test just about everyone.

The Ride

Warm up on tarmac, climbing away from Ullswater. Climb on (mostly) surprisingly gentle grassy tracks up Great Dodd. Then head south, admiring the view, to the descent of your choice. First is Sticks Pass – technical singletrack followed by a steep rocky section. Second, the main track to Glenridding – fast, loose and fun – watch out for walkers. The third option (and the only one to summit Helvellyn), takes a crazily rocky descent to Grizedale Tarn and a hard ride down the valley. Only pick this one if you're good!

Note: *This is not a particularly all-weather route as the climb gets boggy. If you want to ride Helvellyn in the damp, a better way up is the main track (the ride's main descent) from Glenridding. The ride is graded 'Red' for dry conditions. In the wet, or if you take either of the optional descents, it definitely becomes a 'Black' route.*

⚠ Warning: *This is a high mountain – the weather can be bad and visibility poor. Take a map and compass, know what you're doing and go easy on the descents. It's also popular with walkers – lots of people to crash into.* **Take care!**

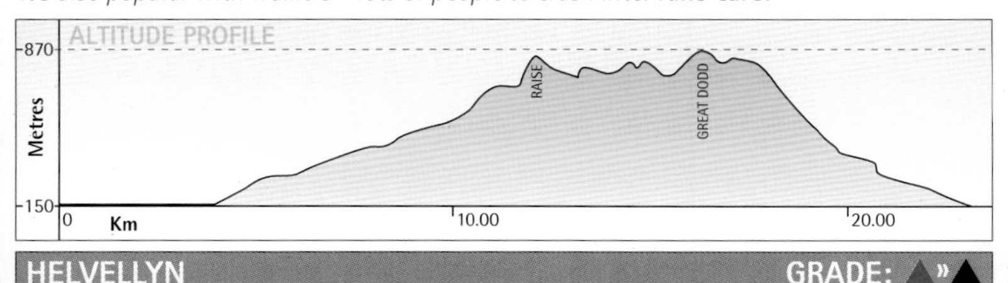

HELVELLYN **GRADE: ▲»▲**

DISTANCE: 22.5KM
TOTAL ASCENT: 1,130M
START/FINISH: CAR PARK IN GLENRIDDING
GRID REFERENCE: NY 385 170
PARKING: PAY AND DISPLAY CAR PARK IN GLENRIDDING
CAFÉ: GLENRIDDING
PUBLIC HOUSE: GLENRIDDING

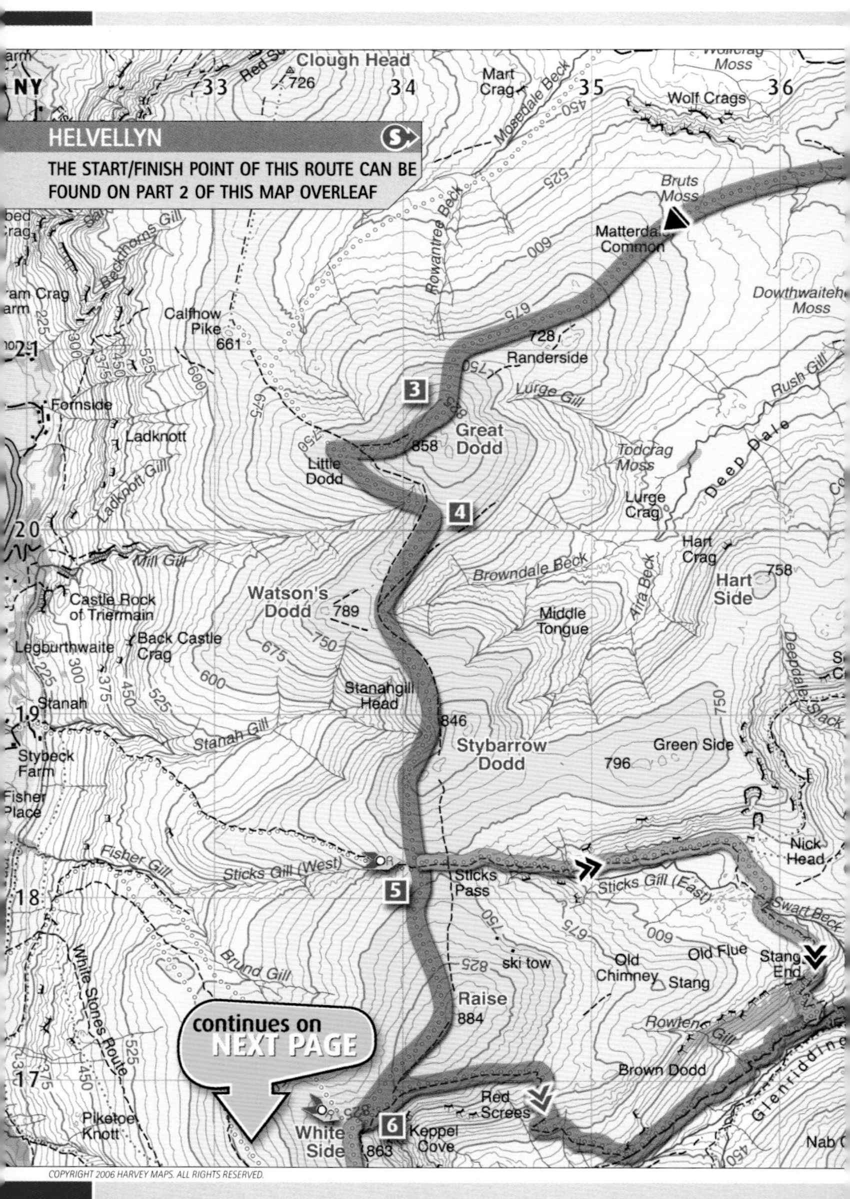
HELVELLYN
THE START/FINISH POINT OF THIS ROUTE CAN BE FOUND ON PART 2 OF THIS MAP OVERLEAF
Clough Head
726
Mart Crag
Mosedale Beck
Wolfcrag Moss
Wolf Crags
Bruts Moss
Matterdale Common
Rowantree Beck
Becthorns Gill
Calfhow Pike
661
Dowthwaitehead Moss
728
Randerside
Lurge Gill
Rush Gill
Fornside
Ladknott
Great Dodd
858
Little Dodd
Ladknott Gill
Todcrag Moss
Deep Dale
Lurge Crag
Mill Gill
Hart Crag
Browndale Beck
Aira Beck
Hart Side
758
Castle Rock of Triermain
Watson's Dodd
789
Middle Tongue
Legburthwaite
Back Castle Crag
Deepdale Slack
Stanah
Stanahgill Head
846
Stanah Gill
Stybarrow Dodd
Green Side
796
Stybeck Farm
Fisher Place
Fisher Gill
Sticks Gill (West)
Sticks Pass
Sticks Gill (East)
Nick Head
Swart Beck
Brund Gill
ski tow
Old Chimney
Old Flue
Stang
Stang End
White Stones Route
Raise
884
Rowten Gill
continues on NEXT PAGE
Brown Dodd
Glenridding
Red Screes
Piketoe Knott
White Side
863
Keppel Cove
Nab C
3
4
5
6
NY
33
34
35
36
21
20
19
18
17
COPYRIGHT 2006 HARVEY MAPS. ALL RIGHTS RESERVED.

Helvellyn (Part 1)

continued from
PREVIOUS PAGE
NY
Raise
884
White Side
863
Red Screes
Keppel Cove
Brown Dodd
Old Chimney
Old Flue
Stang
ski tow
Rowten Gill
Glenridding
Catstycam
890
Helvellyn Lower Man
925
Brown Cove
Swirral Edge
Red Tarn
Helvellyn
950
Striding Edge
Memorial
863
Low Spying How
Whelp Side
Nethermost Cove
Grey Crag
Whelpside Gill
Nethermost Pike
891
High Crag
Middle Tongue
Comb Gill
Comb Crag
Birk Side
Hard Tarn
High Crags
Ruthwaite Cove
Ruthwaite Beck
Ruthwaite Lodge
Eagle Crag
Nethermost Cove Beck
Spout Crag
The Tongue
858
Dollywaggon Pike
Cock Cove
Falcon Crag
Tarn Crag
Deepdale Hause
Birkside Gill
Willie Wife Moor
Steel End
Reggle Knott
Raise Beck
573
Grisedale Tarn
539
Cofa Pike
873
Cawk Cove
Sleet Cove
Piketoe Knott
White Stones Route
Brund Gill
Helvellyn Screes
Long Crag
Dry Gill
Red Tarn Beck
Hole-in-the-
Birkhou
Nab

Helvellyn (Part 2)

Directions – Helvellyn

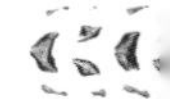

S Head north out of Glenridding on the A592 along the shore of Ullswater, heading for Pooley Bridge. Turn **L** after 3.8km, signed to ***Dockray.*** Once in Dockray, turn **L** just after the bridge, up the lane signed for High Row. At the T-junction, go **SA** over the road and through a gate onto a wide dirt track.

2 Just after crossing a ford, turn **L** (immediately beyond an old fence), onto vague grassy singletrack, which soon becomes more defined. Start to climb. See that big rounded hill ahead of you? That's where you're going. The track is vague and boggy in places. Upon reaching a small rocky summit (unfortunately a false one!), bear **R** and climb steeply.

3 Just before the summit of Great Dodd, the bridleway heads off **R** to join an obvious track. Turn back **L** along it, contouring back along the hillside and up onto the ridge on the other side of the summit. Don't worry if you miss the track and reach the top of the hill, go **SA** over the summit on the obvious path (not a bridleway) and you'll soon rejoin the bridleway.

4 From here, keep going roughly **SA** and south along the ridge. Bear **L** at the fork to run along the left-hand side of the ridge before climbing Stybarrow Dodd and descending fast to a bridleway crossroads.

OptionalRoute

Turn **L** at the crossroads to descend Sticks Pass. Follow the obvious technical single-track to descend to the plateau, and bear to the **R** along its far side, heading for the lowest point. The track becomes more defined and soon becomes very rocky and steep. Descend to a T-junction and turn **L** to continue down the valley to Glenridding.

5 Continue **SA** over the crossroads and climb (carry) up Raise. Go **SA** over the summit and descend to a junction.

Optional Route

Continue **SA**, carry up the narrow ridge ahead and drop down the other side, **ignoring** all tracks to the right. The track forks as it begins to climb. Bear **R** (still climbing) to reach the trig point atop Helvellyn. Continue past this to the cross-shaped shelter and then bear **R** past this to descend a very wide track.

Bear **L** at the bridleway fork, ignoring the narrow footpath climbing steeply straight ahead, and contour to the right around Dollywaggon Pike. (How are your trials skills?) **Take care** – very steep and rocky descent (watch out for the drainage channels that have been built) to Grizedale Tarn. Follow the track to the **L** past the tarn and continue **SA** past the large cairn. The track is not obvious at first. Very hard descent (not all rideable?) along the obvious track down the valley. Stick to the main track, **ignoring** the right turn crossing a side-less wooden bridge. Cross the river and follow the valley out. Turn **R** at the tarmac and **ignore** all turnings until you reach the main road at Grisedale Bridge. Turn **L** back into Glenridding.

6 Turn sharp **L** back on yourself along a wide track. Zig zag down the fast and loose descent, always keeping to the main track and heading down the valley. Turn **L** (keep going **SA**, really) at the T-junction and continue to the youth hostel. Go through the gates, continue to tarmac and keep descending to Glenridding.

Making a day of it

The **Ullswater Singletrack** loop is only a short distance south from Glenridding and would add an excellent couple of hours to your day.

THE FOX

Grizedale & Parkamoor Loop

27km

Introduction

Grizedale Forest is one of the best forests in England for mountain biking. Not only do you have the public rights of way network to go at, but also opened in 2006, The North Face Trail. This is a purpose-built trail similar to those in Scotland and Wales, featuring a few sections of boardwalk and some good singletrack. Don't for a minute think that this is all there is to Grizedale through – it's been a popular riding destination for years due to its extensive network of great bridleways. For the less experienced rider, there are maps available from the visitor centre detailing rides along the forest roads. Watch out for new trails in the future as plans are being made as this book is written!

The Ride

This is quite a day out around Grizedale! With over 900m of climbing, it is not for the faint hearted. Start at the visitor centre and climb the main fire road, which eventually brings you to the start of the bridleway out over Parkamoor. Crossing the moor, a formidable place in poor weather, the route soon joins the 'Land-Rover' track down to High Nibthwaite. From here, a short spin down the road soon finds the route climbing back up on to the moors. The track is firm and fast over to High Ickenthwaite then on to Force Mills and Blind Lane. At Blind Lane the route re-enters the forest to climb over the amusingly named 'Breasty Haw'. A steep descent drops us onto the road to quickly head back into the forest, climbing again for the return leg to the visitor centre.

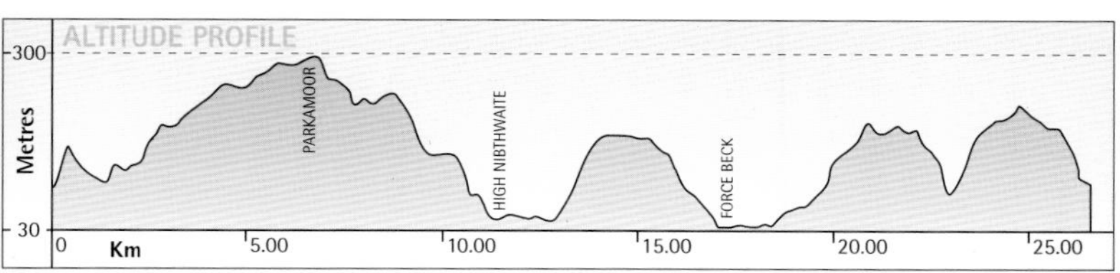

GRIZEDALE & PARKAMOOR LOOP **GRADE: ▲**

DISTANCE: 27KM
TOTAL ASCENT: 947M
START/FINISH: VISITOR CENTRE, GRIZEDALE
GRID REFERENCE: SD 335 943
PARKING: VARIOUS SPOTS AROUND THE VISITOR CENTRE
CAFÉ: VISITOR CENTRE
PUBLIC HOUSE: EAGLES HEAD, SATTERTHWAITE Tel: 01229 860 237

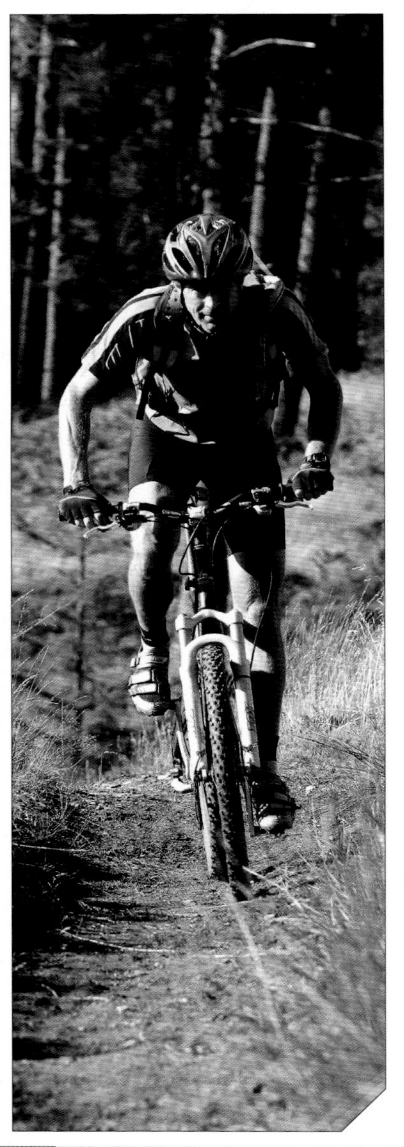

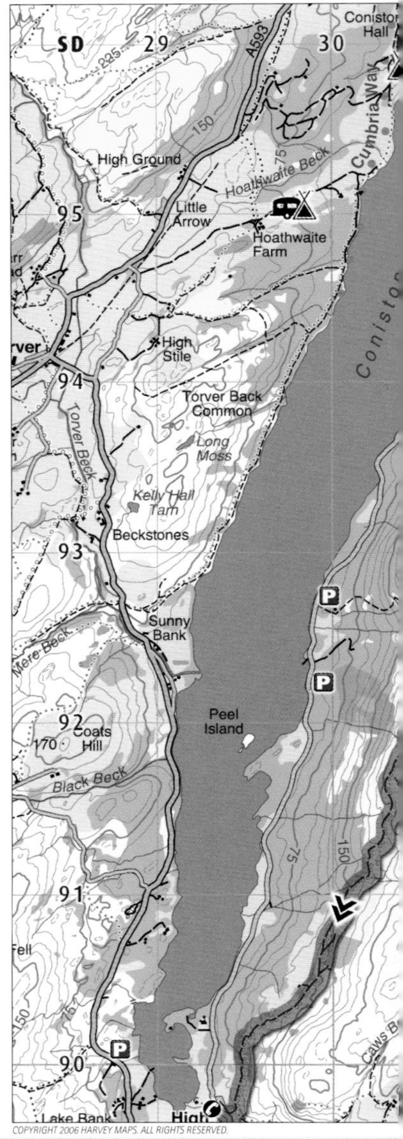

SD
29
30
225
A593
150
High Ground
Hoathwaite Beck
75
Cumbria Way
95
Little
Arrow
Hoathwaite
Farm
High
Stile
94
Torver Back
Common
Torver Beck
Long
Moss
Kelly Hall
Tarn
Beckstones
93
P
Sunny
Bank
Mere Beck
P
Peel
Island
92
Coats
Hill
170
Black Beck
75
150
91
150
75
P
90
Lake Bank

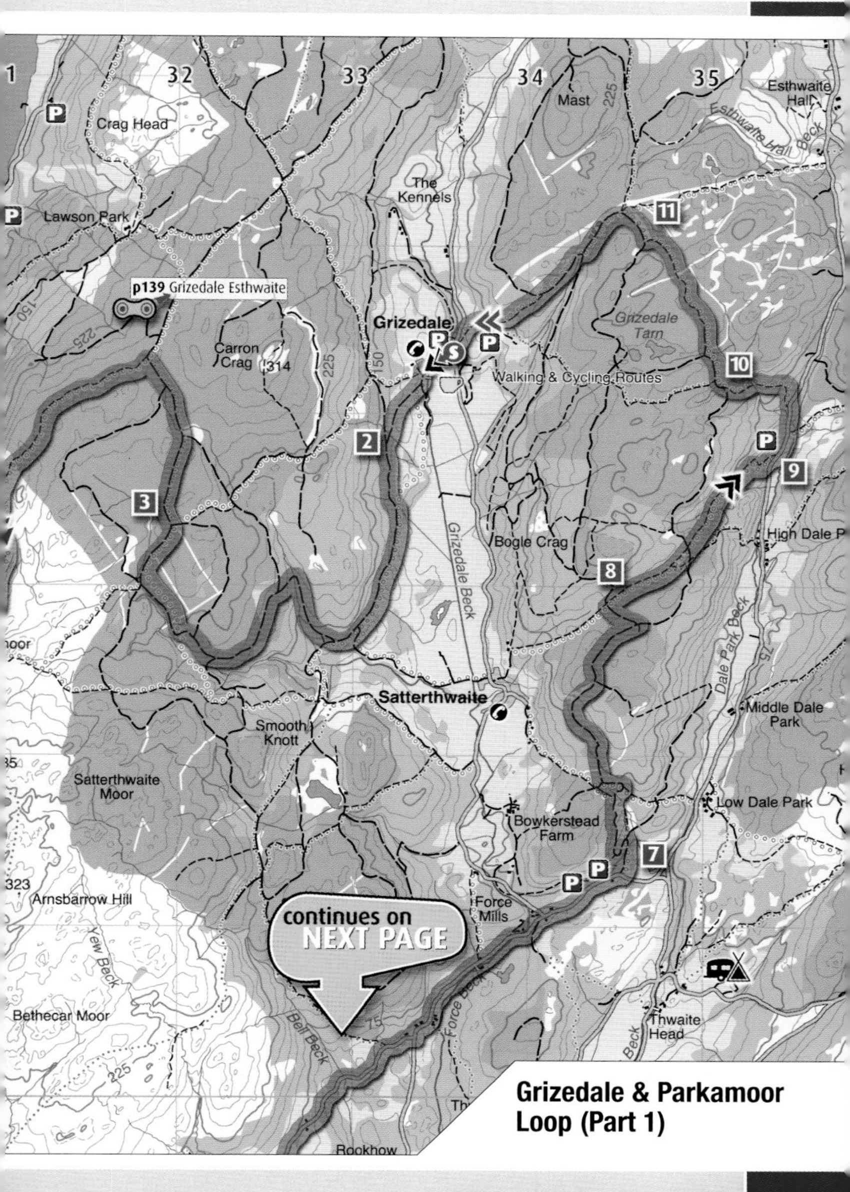

continues on NEXT PAGE

Grizedale & Parkamoor Loop (Part 1)

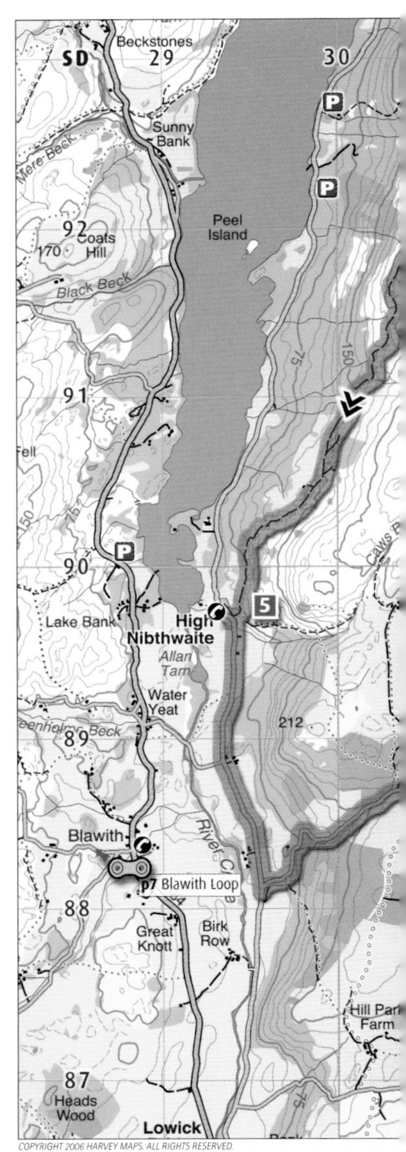

Beckstones
SD
29
30
Sunny Bank
Mere Beck
Peel Island
92
Coats Hill
170
Black Beck
75
150
91
Fell
90
Lake Bank
High Nibthwaite
5
Allan Tarn
Water Yeat
212
89
Blawith
p7 Blawith Loop
88
Great Knott
Birk Row
Hill Park Farm
87
Heads Wood
Lowick

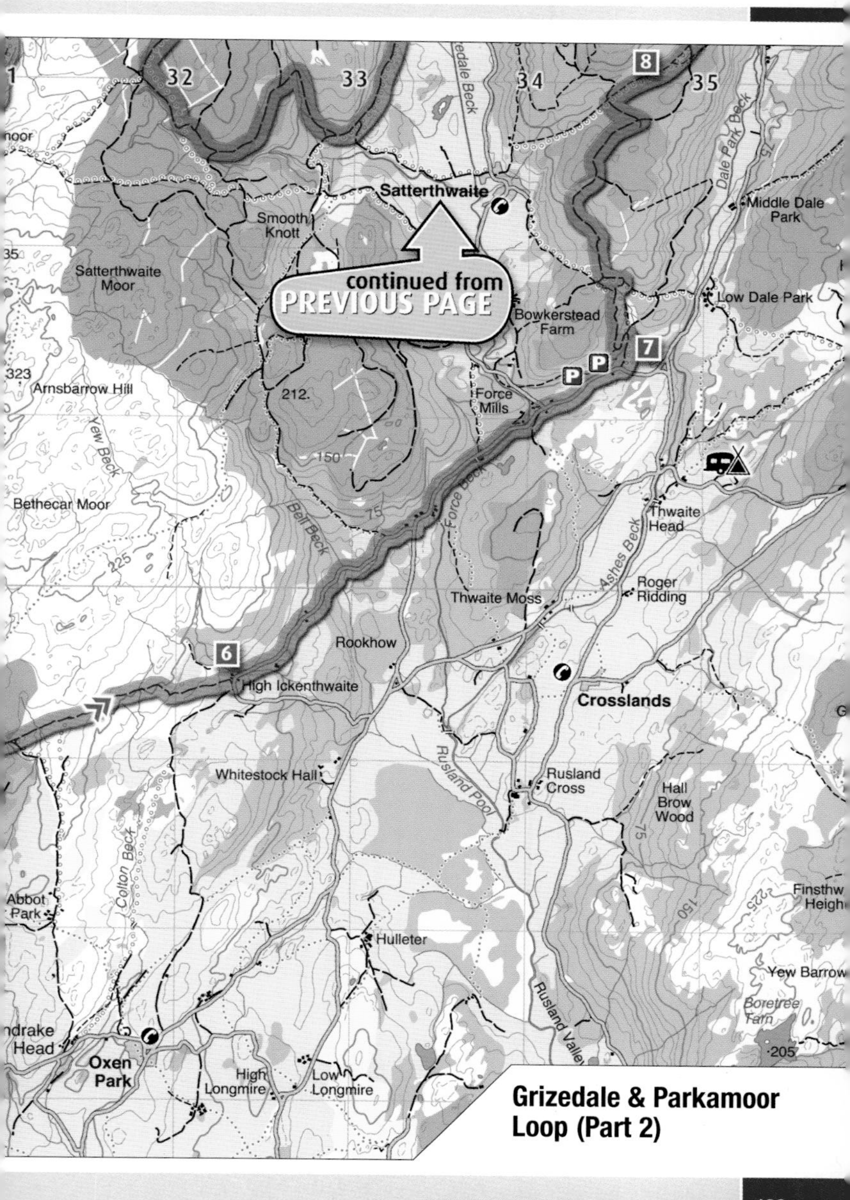

Grizedale & Parkamoor Loop (Part 2)

Directions – Grizedale & Parkamoor Loop

S From the visitor centre farm, head up the main forest road signed *The North Face Trail*. After crossing the cattle grid at the top, **ignore** the TNF trail signs and continue **SA**.

If you are familiar with Grizedale, an alternative route is to follow the TNF trail to the summit of the first singletrack climb, then rejoin the route.

2 Follow the fire road, bearing round to the right to start the climb up to Parkamoor. At the fork, bear **R** uphill and follow the track as it curves back **L** (west) over a stream. Still climbing, bear **L** at the next fork. Continue **SA** on the fire road, **ignoring** a fire road onto the left. At a major fork, bear **L** and continue to a cross roads with a bridleway sign. Turn **R**, still heading uphill (north) and bear **L** at the next junction.

3 Continue **SA** for 2km, **ignoring** bridleways on the right and then left and turn **L** onto an obvious bridleway, signed *Parkamoor*, following it to the gate out onto Parkamoor. Keep to the obvious track through the gate and up a short, steep climb onto a long and fast descent past some recently renovated buildings.

4 Join the track down to a gate at a stream crossing. Climb the hill on the other side to join the wide Land-Rover track. Turn **R** to descend to High Nibthwaite. Take care, as some sections are quite steep and very rocky. All in all this is a cracking descent with something for everyone.

5 Once at the gate at High Nibthwaite, turn **L** onto the road towards Lowick. After approximately 1.5km, turn **L** down a singletrack lane with buildings on either side. Climb steeply up this lane to a gate, **ignoring** a turning on the right to Stock Farm. Continue through the gate bearing **R** and follow the obvious track through another gate to its end at High Ickenthwaite.

6 Turn **L** on the road and continue down to the T-junction at Force Forge. Turn **L** in the direction of Force Mills. Once at Force Mills turn R on a sharp left-hand bend. Continue along this lane, passing Blind Lane car park on the left. Shortly afterwards, turn **L** onto a fire road to climb up onto Breasty Haw.

7 The single bar gate is easily avoided by going round on the right. Follow the forest road to a T-junction and turn **L**. Continue **SA**, ignoring turnings, for about 500m and bear **R** at the fork (a bridleway runs off left). Ignore the next forest road on the right and continue **SA**, **ignoring** turnings for approximately 2km, to Breasty Haws (best name in the forest, although nothing to see). Fork sharp **L** at the junction.

8 After 100m a bridleway crosses the forest road. Turn R out over Breasty Haw. Descend to the forest road and continue **SA** over it for one of the best – and steepest – descents in Grizedale.

9 Join the minor road and turn **L** up a short hill. On the brow of the hill, turn **L** to climb a bridleway. It's steep in places, so you're doing very well if you make it to the top without putting a foot down.

10 At the top turn **R** on the forest road. Follow this to a junction. Turn **R**. This fire road soon turns into a bridleway. Follow this until it joins another fire road after a short sharp climb. Turn **R**.

11 Continue downhill bearing **L** at the sculpture known as The Fox. At the next junction turn **R**, following this fire road. On a right-hand bend turn **L** onto a track. This track starts smoothly but soon becomes very rocky and has claimed many mountain bikers travelling too quickly into the rocky section. So, if you have survived the final descent you will no doubt want a well-earned cuppa in the visitor centre café.

Making a day of it

At the southern end of the route, head west to **Blawith Loop** *(page 7)* for some fine singletrack riding.

ROCKY DESCENT THROUGH FRITH WOOD

Borrowdale Bash

27km

Introduction

This is another popular loop for mountain bikers in the northern half of the lakes. Starting from Keswick, this is a truly all-weather loop with no bogs, on which you'd have to be pretty unlucky to get lost. It's a strange route, with a lot of road work and some lovely easy trails with great views, which would make a great 'blue' grade ride, (beginners' route: keep going straight down the B5289 out of Keswick to Grange and then pick up the end of the ride), but then there are some serious descents, massive road climbs and some technical bits of singletrack thrown in, which boost the route up to a 'black' grade. So it's technical but easy, smooth yet rocky.

The Ride

Take care leaving Keswick – the road down Borrowdale can be busy. A tarmac lane soon leads off to the left, climbing up (and up) past some great viewpoints to Watendlath. Ford the stream and tackle the steep and rocky climb (it is doable) leading up to the top of the first of the route's descents. Drop your saddle (well, I would) and sketch your way down to Rosthwaite. Awesome! Round the end of the valley on the road, grind your way up the beginning of the Honister Pass and turn back on yourself for a fast, open descent, technical singletrack and then a tyre-ripping slate descent into the woods at Grange. A bit of road, 100m of footpath (walk!) and a technical climb lead to some easy undulating singletrack along the western side of Borrowdale, with some lovely views out over Derwent Water. Road leads back to Keswick.

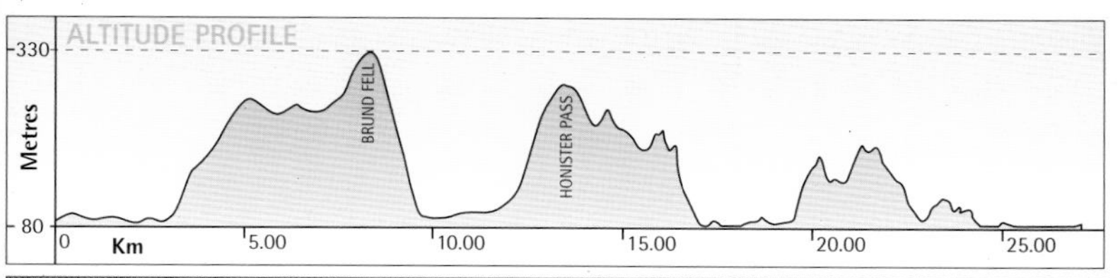

BORROWDALE BASH **GRADE: ▲**

DISTANCE: 27KM

START/FINISH: KESWICK TOWN CENTRE

PARKING: NUMEROUS PAY AND DISPLAYS IN KESWICK

PUBLIC HOUSE: IN VIRTUALLY EVERY VILLAGE ALONG THE ROUTE

TOTAL ASCENT: 950M

GRID REFERENCE: NY 265245

CAFÉ: IN VIRTUALLY EVERY VILLAGE ALONG THE ROUTE

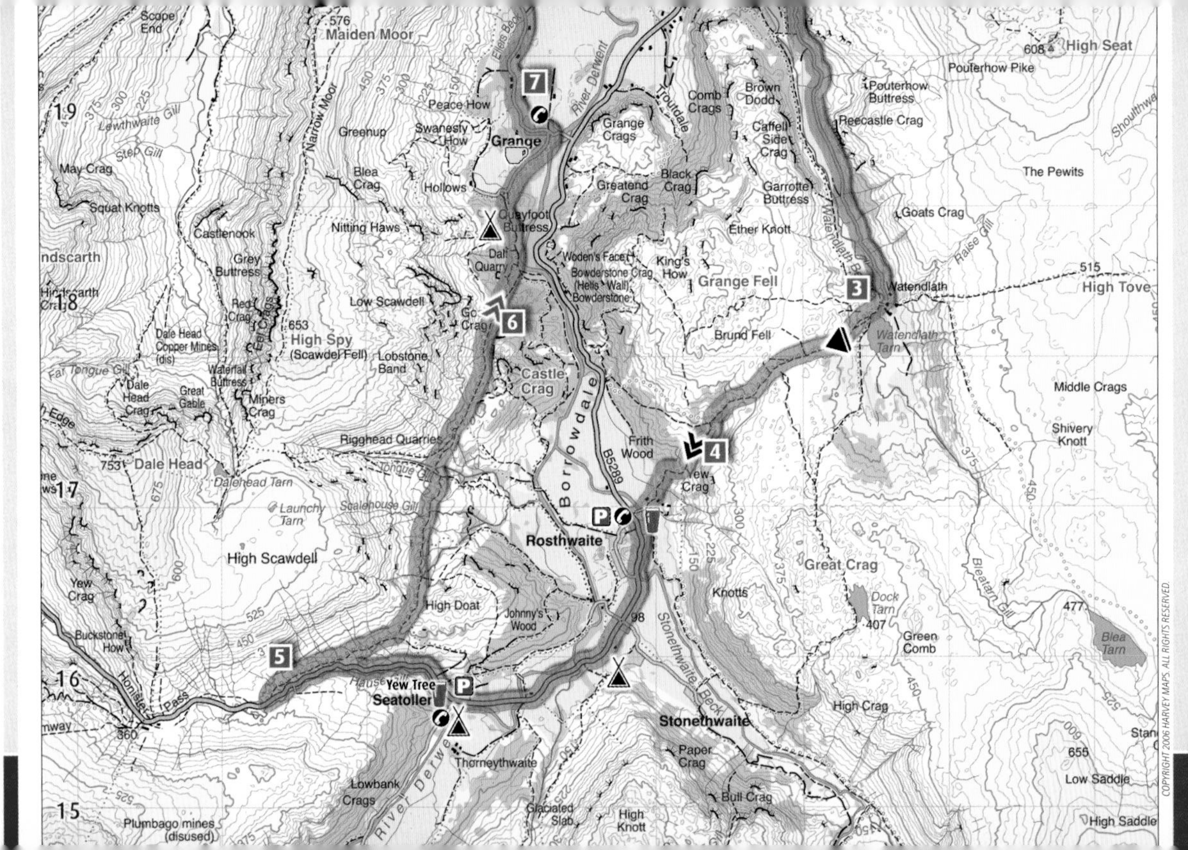

3
4
5
6
7
Scope End
Maiden Moor
Narrow Moor
Peace How
Swanesty How
Grange
Greenup
Blea Crag
Hollows
May Crag
Squat Knotts
Step Gill
Lewthwaite Gill
Castlenook
Grey Buttress
Nitting Haws
Quayfoot Buttress
Dalt Quarry
Low Scawdell
Red Crag
Eel Crags
653
High Spy
(Scawdel Fell)
Lobstone Band
Dale Head Copper Mines (dis)
Far Tongue Gill
Dale Head Crag
Great Gable
Waterfall Buttress
Miners Crag
Castle Crag
Rigghead Quarries
753
Dale Head
Dalehead Tarn
Launchy Tarn
Scaleclose Gill
High Scawdell
Yew Crag
Buckstone How
Honister Pass
360
Yew Tree
Seatoller
High Doat
Johnny's Wood
Thorneythwaite
Lowbank Crags
River Derwent
Plumbago mines (disused)
Glaciated Slab
High Knott
Borrowdale
B5289
Rosthwaite
Frith Wood
Yew Crag
98
Stonethwaite Beck
Stonethwaite
Paper Crag
Bull Crag
Troutdale
Grange Crags
Comb Crags
Brown Dodd
Greatend Crag
Black Crag
Caffell Side Crag
Garrotte Buttress
Woden's Face
Bowderstone Crag
(Hells Wall)
Bowderstone
King's How
Grange Fell
Ether Knott
Brund Fell
Watendlath Beck
Watendlath
Watendlath Tarn
Knotts
Great Crag
Dock Tarn
407
Green Comb
High Crag
608
High Seat
Pouterhow Pike
Pouterhow Buttress
Reecastle Crag
The Pewits
Goats Crag
Raise Gill
515
High Tove
Middle Crags
Shivery Knott
Bleatarn Gill
477
Blea Tarn
655
Low Saddle
High Saddle

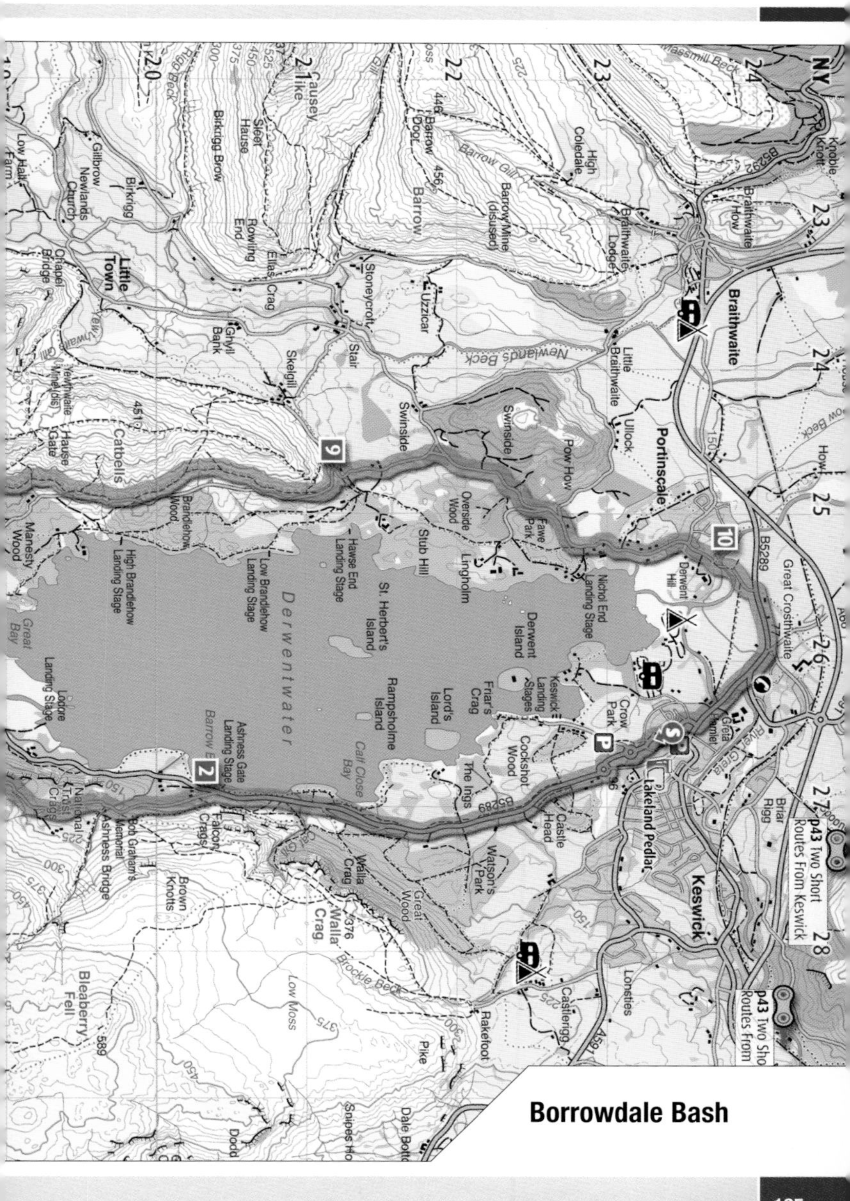

Borrowdale Bash

Directions – Borrowdale Bash

S Follow signs out of Keswick for Borrowdale, following the B5289 south down the valley.

2 After 3km, turn **L** up a dead-end road, signed Watendlath and climb steeply.

Continue on the B5289 for just over 6km and turn **R** over a double-arch stone bride, signed *Grange*. Pick up the route again at **7**).

3 Follow the road to its end in Watendlath and bear **R** where the road splits. Cross the river, go through the gate and keep **R**, heading for the steep stone climb ahead (signed *Bridleway to Rosthwaite*). Climb steeply and follow the track **SA** over the top onto a steep and very rocky descent. Stick to the main track, **ignoring** turnings until the track swings to the left and flattens slightly by a gate in a wall, signed *Bridleway, Rosthwaite*.

4 Follow the track down, through a gate to tarmac and turn **R** over a bridge to the main road. Turn **L**. Go through Seatoller and climb very steeply up the start of the Honister Pass. About 300m after a cattle grid, turn sharp **R** onto an obvious track signed *Bridleway*.

5 **Easy to miss:** Drop back down towards the valley for just over a kilometre looking out for a narrow trail forking left opposite a low wooden sign, signed *Bridleway: Grange*. If you reach some small woods with a gate in the middle, you've gone too far. Continue **SA** through a gate and follow the obvious and technical singletrack across bridges, ignoring all turnings to a fast rocky descent down into the woods.

6 Stick to the main track. Cross a bridge as the track flattens and follow it through the woods to the river. Turn **L** at the river and pick up a good track through a campsite. Follow this to the road, turn **R** and ride into Grange. Turn **L**.

7 Follow the road out of Grange for just over a kilometre to the houses on your left at Manesty. Just past the house and immediately beyond a small wall that juts out towards the road, turn **L** onto the **RH** of two signed footpaths (take the one with the large rock in the middle of the track).

8 Walk along the footpath for a couple of hundred metres to a gate and a bridleway. Climb steeply to a fork by a small cairn and bear **R**, heading for the uphill edge of the woods to your right. Technical singletrack. Keep going **SA** as you leave the woods behind onto an easy and initially grassy track which soon becomes a more obvious track. Follow this as it drops down to the road by a parking bay. After 10m, on the other side of the bay, keep **L** and pick up the bridleway again.

9 At the road, turn **L** (**SA** in effect) round two hairpins, and bear **R** at the next junction, following signs for Keswick.

10 In the village of Portinscale, turn **R** just past the building marked *Tea Rooms and Gift Shop* on the left. Ride to the end of the road and cross the footbridge. Turn **R** at the T-junction with the main road and ride into Keswick.

Making a day of it

This ride uses most of the bridleways in the valley. You could try following the Honister Pass up for a very technical descent down towards Buttermere, but you've have to ride back up again...

WOODLAND SINGLETRACK

Grizedale & Esthwaite

30km

Introduction

This is one of my favourite rides in the forest, as it has everything: technical climbs, singletrack and technical downhill. You will not be disappointed. There's even a bit of tarmac for the hardened roadie! This route will certainly change your views on the forest, if you only thought it was for forestry roads and novice riders. There are 1100m of ascent in the route, so, even though most of the uphill is on forestry roads and tarmac be prepared for tired legs. As ever, the views of the mountains are spectacular, with Wetherlam and Coniston Old Man being of great prominence.

The Ride

The route circumnavigates the forest in a clockwise direction. It starts with forestry roads and singletrack to 'The Fox' before great trails take you over to Esthwaite. Undulating tarmac takes you to the next bridleway, with more stunning downhill to the road at Long Slack. After all the downhills comes an uphill stretch of tarmac. The next bridleway goes through the wood yard before climbing steeply onto Satterthwaite via the downhill at Breasty Haw. It crosses over to the west side of Grizedale and climbs, mainly on fire roads, before one of the best downhills in the forest, Lawson Park, and of course the climb back, before a final technical downhill and a saunter back to Moor Top.

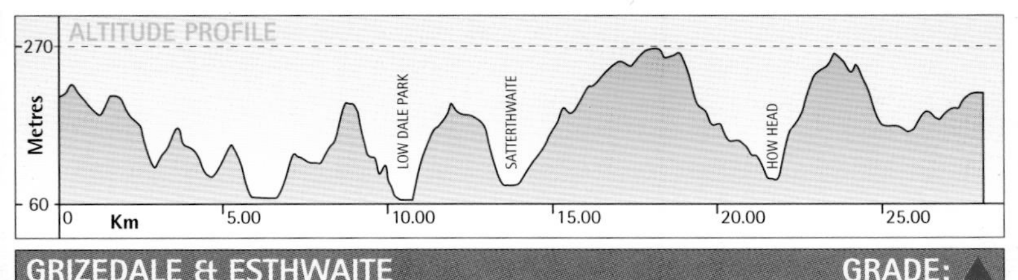

GRIZEDALE & ESTHWAITE — **GRADE: ▲**

DISTANCE: 30KM
TOTAL ASCENT: 1,100M
START/FINISH: MOOR TOP
GRID REFERENCE: SD 342 964
PARKING: MOOR TOP CAR PARK
CAFÉ: FORESTRY VISITOR CENTRE Tel: 01229 860 010
PUBLIC HOUSE: EAGLES HEAD IN SATTERTHWAITE Tel: 01229 860 237

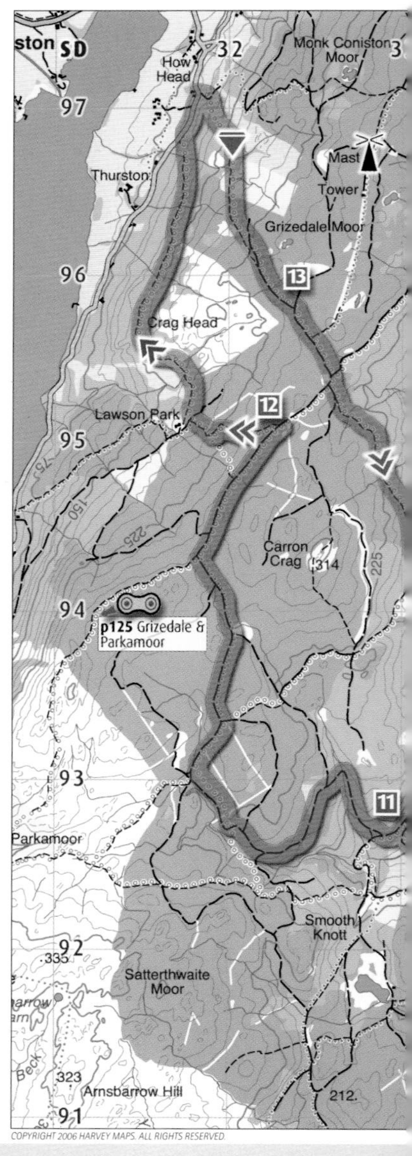
ston
SD
32
How Head
Monk Coniston Moor
97
Thurston
Mast
Tower
Grizedale Moor
96
13
Crag Head
Lawson Park
12
95
150
225
Carron Crag
314
225
94
p125 Grizedale & Parkamoor
93
11
Parkamoor
Smooth Knott
92
335
Satterthwaite Moor
Beck
323
Arnsbarrow Hill
212.
91

Grizedale & Esthwaite

Directions – Grizedale & Esthwaite

S Turn **R** along the main road from the Moor Top car park. Within 50m, turn **L** onto a fire road and then turn **L** again at the next junction, heading east. Follow the forest road as it swings south, and then, on a sharp left hand bend, turn **R** onto a bridleway. Follow this to a second forest road and turn **L**. (The 'Fox' is off to the right if you want to have a look.)

2 After the initial rise, this track gives a fine downhill that is not without technical interest. Continue to the road.

3 Turn **R** along the road, climbing steeply south. **Easy to miss:** after 1.7km, pass a bridleway on the right, descend steeply and, as the forest opens out, turn **L** onto a bridleway signed *Long Slack*. Testing climbing to a gate. Go through the gate and follow the track round to the right. Fork **L** at the junction of two gates (marked with a bridleway sign).

4 Continue to climb, going **SA** over the fire road and climb for a short distance, before a great technical downhill. At the road, turn **R** and head south south-east.

5 Follow the road for 2.3km, climbing steeply in places. Just after the Grathwaite sign, turn **R** at Black Brows Close (sawmill) and follow the bridleway through the sawmill yard. This is a working yard so **please take care!** As the track splits, fork **R** and climb very steeply to Hazel Seat Wood and a rewarding downhill.

6 At the forest road, go **SA** (slightly **R**), following bridleway signs. Within 50m, turn **R** through a deer gate onto a bridleway signed *Low Dale Park*. Technical single track leads to another deer gate. Go through this, through another gate and follow the bridleway down to Low Dale Park Farm and a metalled road which leads through the farm buildings.

7 Turn **L** at the T-junction with the road, then, after 100m, turn **R** onto another bridleway and either be brave and get wet fording the stream or use the footbridge and stay dry.

8 The bridleway heads uphill before it joins a fire road. (Although the bridleway continues straight ahead on the other side of the fire road and looks like a short cut on the map, it is not.) Turn **L** (south) along the fire road and take the next **R** (heading north) back on yourself.

9 Continue **SA** along this forest track, **ignoring** turnings, for about 500m and bear **R** at the fork (a bridleway runs off left). **Ignore** the next forest road on the right and continue **SA**, **ignoring** turnings for approximately 2km, to Breasty Haw (best name in the forest, although nothing to see). Fork **L** at the junction and, after 100m, turn **L** onto a bridleway (there is a signed bridleway to the right here), heading south-west. Join a metalled road that leads to a T-junction with the road through Satterthwaite.

10 Turn **R**, then quickly **L** onto a signed bridleway, heading west north-west on a partially metalled road to a gate. Just before entering the forest, go through another gate to a T-junction and turn **L**.

11 At the fork, bear **R** uphill and follow the track as it curves back **L** (west) over a stream. Still climbing, bear **L** at the next fork. Continue **SA** on the fire road, **ignoring** a fire road on the left. At a major fork, bear **L** and continue to a cross roads with a bridleway sign. Turn **R**, still heading uphill (north) and bear **L** at the next junction. Continue **SA** for 2km, **ignoring** fire roads on the right and left, a bridleway to Parkamoor on the left and then another fire road on the left before eventually turning **L** onto a bridleway as the hill levels out to a plateau.

12 Now it's downhill for the next 2.5km so enjoy! At the buildings at Lawson Park, keep **R** on a gated track to join a metalled road on the east shore of Lake Coniston. Turn **R** (heading north), for 500m and turn **R** onto a bridleway at Bank Grounds, signed *Satterthwaite/Grizedale*. Attack the uphill boulder field (impressive if you can ride the first section), and, with tired legs, join another fire road, turning **R**.

13 Pass another fire road on the left and bear **L** at the fork. As the fire road bears to the right after 50m, go **SA** onto a bridleway for a stunning downhill. Join a fire road and turn **L**, **ignoring** all turnings for a 3km undulating amble back to Moor Top.

Making a day of it

Explore the forest! We've suggested two other routes in the area, but it's full of great trails that can be linked in any way you fancy.

LEAVING THE CAR PARK

Skiddaw Loop

44km

Introduction

The bridleways around Skiddaw have long been popular with mountain bikers, and for good reason. They manage to strike a nice balance between being too hard for the less experienced and too boring for the pros. This loop takes in the popular trails and combines them with some less-used trails to form a loop with the least amount of road work possible. There are some great views and parts of the ride have a real wilderness feel to them. You'll need to watch out in the wet, as some of the more technical sections get very slippery, and you should take a map and compass in bad weather, but otherwise this is a relatively all-weather route.

The Ride

The fantastic bridleway clinging to the side of Lonscale Fell is technical in places, slippery in the wet, and the big drop can put people off... but it's fun and leads to Skiddaw House, from where the route descends a rutted and lumpy bridleway to Mosedale. The terrain eases and speeds increase as you reach a track and then tarmac. A stone track heads west from Calebreck over bleak fells and through old mine works. A fast, grassy descent leads to Fell Side and a short tarmac spin gives way to a green lane and another fast and grassy descent. More road work passes pink- (or is it salmon?), straw- and peppermint-coloured houses before reaching the steep track up past the atmospheric Dash Falls. A straight-line descent and short climb lead back to Skiddaw House and the outward route.

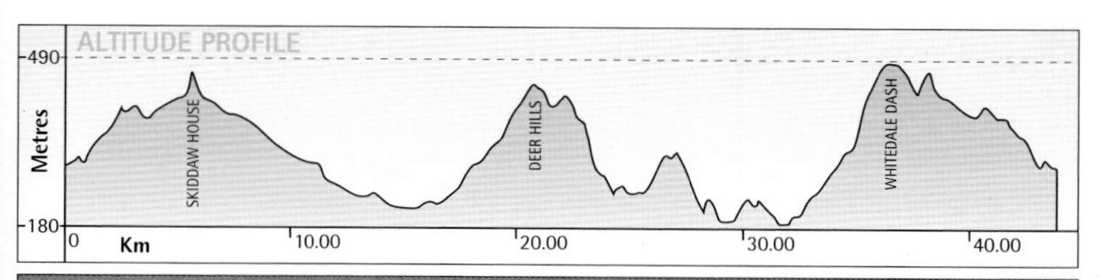

SKIDDAW LOOP — **GRADE:** ▲

DISTANCE: 44KM

START/FINISH: CAR PARK ABOVE LATRIGG

PARKING: FREE CAR PARK

PUBLIC HOUSE: DOWN THE HILL IN KESWICK

TOTAL ASCENT: 1,250M

GRID REFERENCE: NY 281 254

CAFÉ: LOTS OF NICE PICNIC SPOTS...

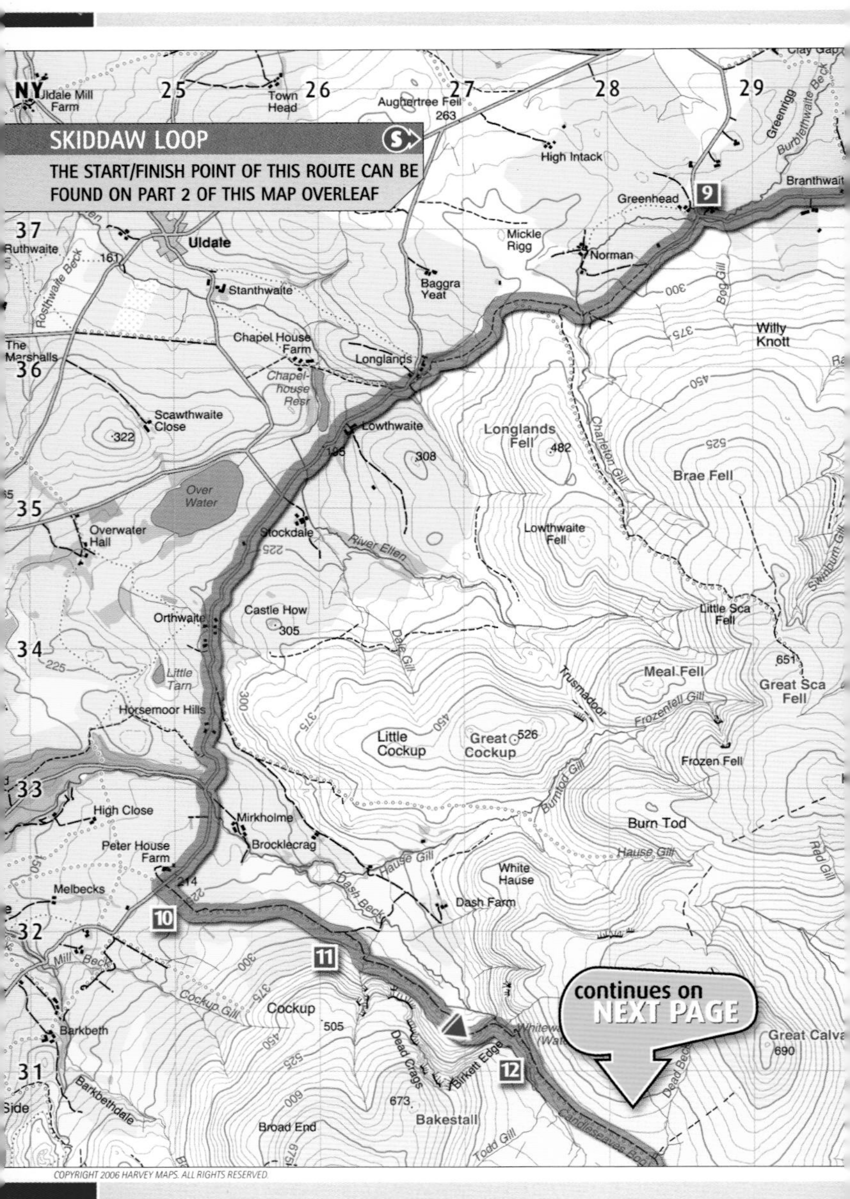
SKIDDAW LOOP
THE START/FINISH POINT OF THIS ROUTE CAN BE FOUND ON PART 2 OF THIS MAP OVERLEAF
Uldale
Longlands Fell
Brae Fell
Great Sca Fell
Little Cockup
Great Cockup
Cockup
Bakestall
Great Calva
Over Water
continues on NEXT PAGE

Skiddaw Loop (Part 1)

NY
25
26
27
28
29
31
30
29
28
27
26
25
Dash Farm
Little Calva
642
Great Calva
690
Cockup
505
Barkbeth
Barkbethdale
Cockup Gill
Mill Beck
Whitewater Dash (Waterfall)
Dead Crags
Birkett Edge
Dead Beck
673
Bakestall
Broad End
Candleseaves Bog
Todd Gill
Barkbeth Gill
Great Knott
Hare Crag
The Edge
Southerndale
Southerndale Beck
River Caldew
Far Grain
931
Skiddaw
Skiddaw House
Sale How
690
Ullock Pike
Stile Gill
Salehow Beck
Slat Gill
733
Long Side
Carl Side
746
Carside Tarn
Broad End
Skiddaw Little Man
865
Pike Sike
Jenkin Hill
Longside Wood
Gable Gill
Slades Beck
491
Dodd
Grey Crags
Howgill Tongue
714
Lonscale Fell
Dodd Wood
Doups
Lyzzick Hall
River Derwent
Millbeck
78
123
Applethwaite Gill
Whit Beck
p43 Two Short Routes From Keswick
Ghyll
Low Grove Farm
Applethwaite
Underscar
Monument
New Close Piggery
Ormathwaite
Lonscale
Thrushwood
Latrigg
367
Spooney Green Lane
Brundholme Wood
River Greta
Bog House
Pow Beck
How
A66
A591
10
11
12
3
2
S
P

Skiddaw Loop (Part 2)

Directions – Skiddaw Loop

S Leave the car park through the gate at the far end from the road, immediately turning **L**. Go **SA** through the next gate and bear **R** as the track forks just after a third gate. Follow the obvious track as it contours around the side of Lonscale Fell.

2 As the track leaves the hillside, keep going **SA** up the head of the valley. **Ignore** the turning to the right just after the little ruined hut.

3 Stick to the obvious track until you reach Skiddaw House, passing alongside the wall in front of the building. As the wall ends, turn sharp **R**, heading downhill alongside another wall.

4 Follow the track (vague in places) along the left-hand side of the valley, **ignoring** all turnings until it widens and the going eases. Continue along the wide track to the road and follow this **SA** down the valley.

5 Turn **L** at the T-junction in Mosedale and follow the road north. After 2.5km the road bends to the right, with a lone chevron sign warning drivers. Continue **SA** onto a track to cut the corner, and **SA** along the road as the track ends.

6 After a further 1.5km the road reaches a small layby just before a cattle grid. Turn **L** up the good track in the layby (**ignoring** the grassy bridleway going off left immediately after the start of the track). Follow this obvious track past two sets of old mine workings.

7 After the second old mine working, follow the track up a short, steep and straight climb and go **SA** over the vague crossroads just beyond. After 150m the track appears to end. Turn sharp **R** onto a vague grassy track to descend and climb over the small hill to the right. The track becomes more obvious as you crest the hill.

8 Descend fast, **ignoring** all turnings, to a T-junction with a loose stone track running alongside a wall. Turn **R** and descend through a gate to the road. Turn **L**.

9 After 2km, turn **L** over a small bridge with white railings onto a dead-end lane. Follow the lane and, as it swings right to a gate, continue **SA** onto a dirt track. Follow this to a gate just beyond a house and go through this to the road. Turn **L**.

10 Continue for 4km, passing two lanes on the right as you go. About 750m after the second turning, pass Peter House Farm in a small wood. Just beyond it, turn **L** onto a tarmac lane signed *Bridleway to Skiddaw House.*

11 Follow the lane for 1.5km until a wide stone track forks off **R**, signed *Bridleway to Skiddaw House and Threlkeld* on a large rock. Climb steeply up past Dash Falls to a gate.

12 Go through the gate and keep following the wide track, **ignoring** all turnings, until it descends and climbs to Skiddaw House. Bear **L** and then **R** to pass in front of the house and re-join your outward route.

Making a day of it

The **Lonscale Fell Loop** on *page 43* makes a great alternative start to this ride, adding a little extra distance and a final fast descent into Keswick.

GRASSY RIDING NEAR ST. PETER'S CHURCH

High Street North

30km

Introduction

A classic for mountain bikers! A trip up High Street is almost less about the riding and more about a big day out in the hills. After pushing or carrying your bike up a huge hill, the undulating ride along the northern half of High Street offers great views in every direction. It's a similar case on the return leg up Boredale – some carrying, but in a lovely setting and the rewards are some great views. It's not all about the views and 'getting out there' though. The descent from Loadpot Hill is seriously fast in places and features some flat-out singletrack and the downhill run from the top of Boredale is as fast as you dare!

The Ride

You may as well leave the car park in the granny gear as you'll probably only find a couple of hundred metres of flat/downhill riding in the first three kilometres! Grind your way up toward Hayeswater on a good track before swinging onto grass. The next up to The Knott is just that, but once you're up, you're up, and there are some great 360° views of virtually everywhere in the Lakes (almost!). Undulate along the ridge to the fast and swoopy descent off the end. Turn left towards Ullswater and speed down to Howtown and a choice of return routes: either climb up Boredale (with a push at the top) and speed down the other side, or pick your way along the technical bridleway along skirting around the side of Ullswater. Easy tracks lead back to Low Hartsop.

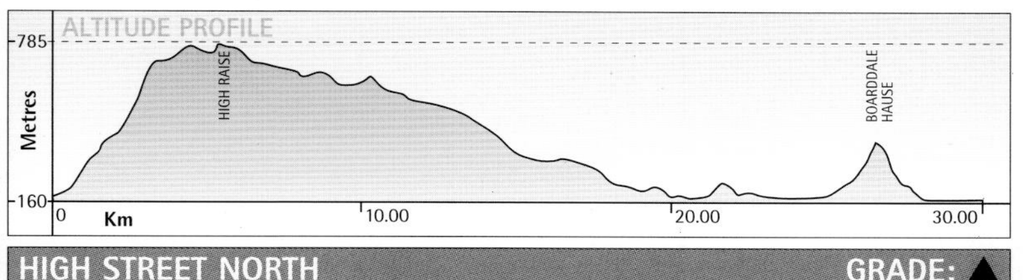

HIGH STREET NORTH — **GRADE: ▲**

DISTANCE: 30KM
START/FINISH: LOW HARTSOP
PARKING: CAR PARK IN LOW HARTSOP
PUBLIC HOUSE: NONE ON THE RIDE
TOTAL ASCENT: 1,220M
GRID REFERENCE: NY 410 130
CAFÉ: SANDWICH TIME

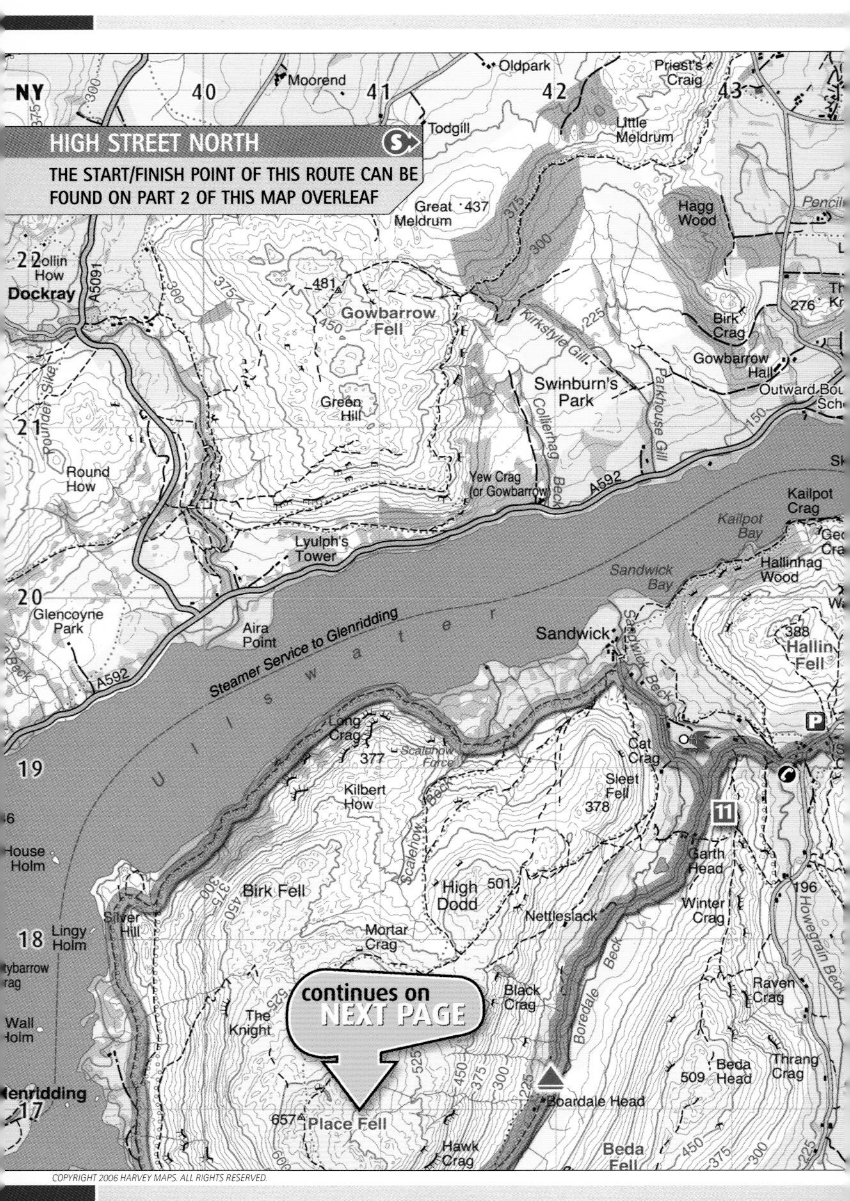

continues on NEXT PAGE

High Street North (Part 1)

Black Crag
The Knight
40
41
42
43
Boredale
Crag
Beda Head
Thrang Crag
509
Boardale Head
657
Place Fell
Hawk Crag
Round How
Redgate Gill
Beda Fell
Boardale
Dalehead
Grisedale Bridge
Patterdale
Rooking Gill
Bedafell Knott
Red Scar
Blue Gill
Goldrill Bridge
Chapel in the Hause
393
Mill Moss
Stonebarrow Gill
Crookabeck
531
Freeze Beck
Bannerdale
Beck
Rake Crag
Heck Cove
Heck Beck
Stoney Rigg
Arnison Crag
Goldrill Beck
577
Heck Crag
Beckstones
434
Angletarn Pikes
567
Dubhow Crag
Dubhow Beck
Dubhow Gill
Yewgrove Gill
Bridgend
Buck Crag
Fall Crag
Cat Crag
Angle Tarn
Deepdale Beck
571
Deepdale Park
Low Wood
Calf Close
Lingy Crag
Brock Crags
Satura Crag
697
561
Eden Beck
A592
Caiftgate Gill
Low Hartsop
Prison Crag
Prison Gill
Sulphury Gill
Hayeswater Gill
Bleaberry Knott
Brothers Water
The Knott
422
Threshthwaite Glen
Hayeswater
Low Wood Top
Hartsop Hall
Brotherswater Hotel
618
Hartsop Dodd
697
Gray Crag
Pasture
Dovedale
Hartsop Beck
Caudale Bridge
Raven Crag

High Street North (Part 2)

Directions – High Street North

S From the parking area, go through the gate at the end (signed *Hayeswater*). The track starts as dirt (briefly) before becoming tarmac for a while. At the fork immediately after the cattle grid, bear **R** and descend to cross a bridge and start the first part of the climb proper.

2 The bridleway crosses the river and runs up the hillside for a couple of hundred metres before reaching Hayeswater, but it's hard to spot. The easiest route is to continue to Hayeswater, turning **L** as you reach it to cross the footbridge – although this short section is a footpath, so act appropriately.

3 Keep going **SA** up the massive grassy hillside in front of you. The track is vague at first, but becomes more obvious higher up, crossing a broken wall and bearing to the right, becoming more rideable as it does so. (If in doubt, you are heading up onto the blunt ridge, and then to the left-hand side of, and behind, the knobby hill on your right.)

4 The track meets a wall and bears left. Follow it to a junction with a cairn and turn sharp **L** to climb up to Rampsgill Head. At the summit (jagged rocks), turn **L** and continue **SA**, descending and climbing onto High Raise. Drop down to a wall and follow it to the **R**. At the corner, cross the stile and continue. Go through a gate.

5 Follow the vague track, keeping the fence to your left and climb. Descend through a gap in the wall.

6 Climb and descend again and then, just before climbing onto Loadpot Hill, (recognisable by the trig point on the summit), the bridleway bears **L**, passing the hill on its western side. If you miss the track and climb to the summit, you're on a footpath, but you can descend meet the bridleway again by continuing **SA** over the hill.

7 Begin to descend. You'll reach a fork after about 1km – **ignore** the left-hand fork (which is the more obvious track and is probably covered in tyre tracks), and bear **R** onto narrower, grassy track and continue to descend.

8 You will eventually reach a T-junction with an obvious track as the gradient eases (hill ahead). Turn **L** and follow this track as it weaves its way towards Ullswater. Follow the track as it becomes more defined for a fast descent.

9 Bear **L** where the track forks (the obvious track descends to the right) and ride to a gate by a house (signed Cyclists, please walk). Follow the track around to the **R** and turn **L** through a gate with a bridleway sign.

10 Cross the river and head up a short climb to a 4-way sign. Go **SA** signed *Public Bridleway Martindale House* along a grassy track that contours, descends and climbs. Keep going **SA** (**ignore** a left turn just before the second steep climb). Drop down to the church and the road. Turn **L** and then **R** at the junction, following signs for Sandwick.

Optional Route

Follow the hairpin round to the right and continue down the road. At the car park, turn **L** onto a bridleway signed *Bridlepath to Patterdale*. This soon turns to technical singletrack running around the edge of Ullswater. It eventually widens. Go **SA** through the gate at Side Farm and **SA** onto tarmac through the next gate. Follow the road round to the **R** and turn **L** at the main road. Ride to the houses at Bridgend and turn **L** onto a signed bridleway just before the last house. Follow this bridleway through gates, across fields and over the river to a good track. Turn **R** back to Low Hartsop.

11 Go **SA** at the hairpin, signed *Patterdale, Footpath Only*. At the end of the road, go **SA** through gates onto the obvious track. Steady climbing leads up a quiet valley with great views. You'll have to carry the last bit of the climb.

12 Follow the track round to the **R**, and then **SA** (south-west) across the plateau you have reached, heading for the lowest point its 'open' (western) edge. **Ignore** turnings until you reach a small, smooth, flattish area. Continue **SA** across this (there's a bit of a gully on the left) and a wide, loose track will appear, descending very steeply towards Patterdale.

13 At the bottom, turn **L** (**SA**) along the wide track. At the road, turn **L** and climb back to Low Hartsop.

Making a day of it

There are loads of options here. Ride the **Ullswater singletrack** *(page 51)*, continue south to ride the full **High Street** or explore the bridleways at the northern end of the ride.

Walna Scar

21km

Introduction

This is a route for experienced mountain bikers, as it involves crossing high mountain country on very difficult technical ascents and descents. Expect to shoulder your bike, but believe me, it's all worth it in the end as you nail one of the classic Lakeland passes. This route only takes in half of the full Walna Scar road. If you want to ride the entire thing (and it's well worth it) turn to page 57 and link this ride to the Seathwaite – Dunnerdale route, giving a great ride linking some fun trails from Coniston to Dunnerdale and then a return route up and over the full Walna Scar Road.

The Ride

We start in Coniston at the ferry terminal, mainly because the café there comes highly recommended – especially in winter when you're guaranteed a table! The route heads out towards the Coniston Hall Campsite then on to Torver. Once through Torver, some pleasant lanes climb steeply into woods and drop to the River Lickle via some sweet singletrack. An undulating climb on the west bank of the river leads to some seriously technical climbing – expect to shoulder your bike – up to meet the Walna Scar Road, which it follows up and over Walna Scar itself. It's then downhill all the way back to Coniston on this classic pass. For a completely different, but equally good challenge, try the route in reverse.

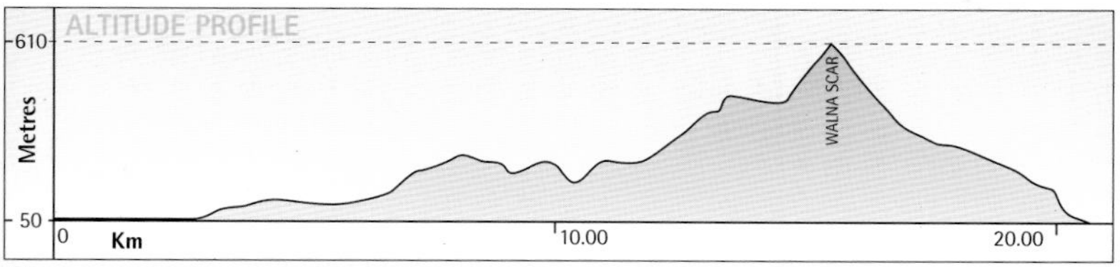

WALNA SCAR **GRADE: ▲**

DISTANCE: 21KM
TOTAL ASCENT: 807M
START/FINISH: CAR PARK AT FERRY TERMINAL, END OF LAKE ROAD
GRID REFERENCE: SD 308 970
PARKING: FERRY TERMINAL OR VARIOUS CAR PARKS IN CONISTON
CAFÉ: BLUEBIRD CAFÉ, CONISTON Tel: 01539 441 649
PUBLIC HOUSE: VARIOUS IN CONISTON

SD
Grassguards
23
24
25
26
Seathwaite Fells
Green How Top
778
High Tongue
232
150
Tongue House
Long House
Hollin How
97
Wallbarrow Gorge
Hollin House Tongue
Low Crag
Peel Crag
Tarn Beck
Seathwaite Buttress
Turner Hall Farm
Moss Crag
Long House Gill
Brown Pike
682
8
Walna Scar Road
96
Seathwaite
Pub Name
Gobling Beck
Wash Dub Beck
White Pike
White Maiden
608
7
525
450
High Greens
95
Old Park Beck
Pikes
375
Caw
529
Natty Bridge
Broughton Moor Quarry
300
94
385
Fox Haw
p93 Broughton Moor & Seathwaite
6
Stephenson Ground
332
5
4
93
Jackson Ground
p57 Seathwaite – Dunnerdale
Raven's Crag
Appletree Worth Beck
Carter Ground
Town End
225

Buckbarrow Crag
Quarry
The Bell
Miners Bridge
Guards Wood
B5285
803
Coniston Old Man
Scrow Beck
Dixon Ground
The Black Bull
Coniston
Quarries (disused)
9
Cat Bank
2
Bluebird Café
Little Arrow Moor
Walna Scar Road
Boo Tarn
Heathwaite
Haws Bank
Coniston Hall
A593
Tranearth Beck
Cumbria Way
High Ground
Hoathwaite Beck
Little Arrow
Hare Crags
Hoathwaite Farm
Scarr Head
3
Coniston Water
Under Crag
Torver
High Stile
Brocklebank Ground
Torver Back Common
Torver Beck
Moor Farm
Long Moss
Souterstead
Kelly Hall Tarn
Hazel Hall
Beckstones
Parkamoor
Sunny Bank
Torver Low Common
Mere Beck
Ground
Walna Scar

Directions – Walna Scar

S From the ferry car park, go back towards Coniston, go over the bridge and, on the right-hand bend, go **L** through the double gate onto the cycleway to Torver.

2 Follow the cycleway to Coniston Hall National Trust Campsite. Continue through the campsite staying on the metalled road. Bear **L** at the fork toward the lake (a sign says *No camping beyond this point*). Pick up the cycleway again at the next gate, continuing through the field to a gate, following signs to Torver.

3 The track joins tarmac, which leads to a T-junction. Turn **R** and ride to the main road, passing over the old railway. Turn **L** towards Torver, ride through the village and turn **R** 1.5km after the village to climb steeply up a narrow lane.

4 At the forest, turn **R** through a gate at the forestry sign *Broughton Moor*. Descend to a right-hand bend and start to climb. **Ignore** the forest road on the left. On the brow of the climb turn **L** onto a bridleway to descend superb singletrack. At the junction with the forest road below, turn **L**. The fire road descends to cross a concrete bridge and then to climb steeply to another fire road. Turn **L** and then **R (easy to miss)** onto singletrack just after a right-hand bend. Follow this superb singletrack to drop steeply to yet another fire road.

5 Turn **R** then immediately **L** down a bridleway. Continue through the gate to the lane and turn **R**, crossing the bridge and climbing steeply to the farm (Stephenson Ground).

6 At the farm, turn **R** through a gate, signed *Bridleway*. After passing through the gate continue **SA** towards Walna Scar. (**Ignore** the bridleway on the left). The track becomes more arduous the further you go, but don't be put off – it's worth it! The bridleway follows a stream some metres below. After passing through the second gate just after a path junction the trail becomes more technical with a few dismounts likely unless you're a real talent! Eventually the bridleway crosses the stream to meet with the path/bridleway on the opposite side. Continue climbing **SA**. Bear **R** at the next path junction.

7 The ground becomes increasingly boggy, the worst of which can be avoided by taking the higher ground, especially in winter when keeping your feet dry is preferable! Skirt the bottom of a small crag before eventually reaching some ruined buildings (the area was once quarried for slate). Follow the obvious path between the buildings before heading out over the fell again.

8 There are a few choices of path but stay high, eventually meeting the well-maintained Walna Scar Road, now so big I'm sure it's visible from Outer Space! Turn **R** and climb steeply to the summit. It may be clear, it may not. How much did you ride? None of that matters now as the rest of the route is downhill into Coniston. How fast you go depends on you(!) but **be warned**, this road moves and changes according to how much rain there's been. Expect the unexpected – and walkers. The descent is steep, rocky and loose, has a huge drop-off and is worth every painful pedal and step you took to get to the top!

9 Eventually the 'road' reaches a car park and a gate. Continue **SA** onto a metalled lane which leads down into Coniston. At the very bottom continue **SA** over the main road down Lake Road to return to the car park at the ferry terminal.

Making a day of it

If you want to ride the full Walna Scar road (you do!) then pick up the **Seathwaite** route *(page 57)* half way through and use follow it to the top of Walna Scar.

SECTION 4

Killers

Character building...

We wouldn't go so far as to say that these loops could kill you, but they won't be much fun if you're not prepared. Allow plenty of time; stock up well on the calories and make sure you're firing on all four cylinders.

Giro
THOMSON

KULA
BOMBER
PRO

Killers route finder

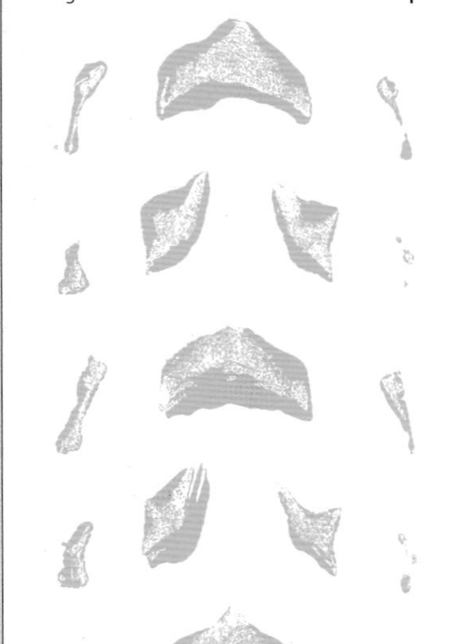

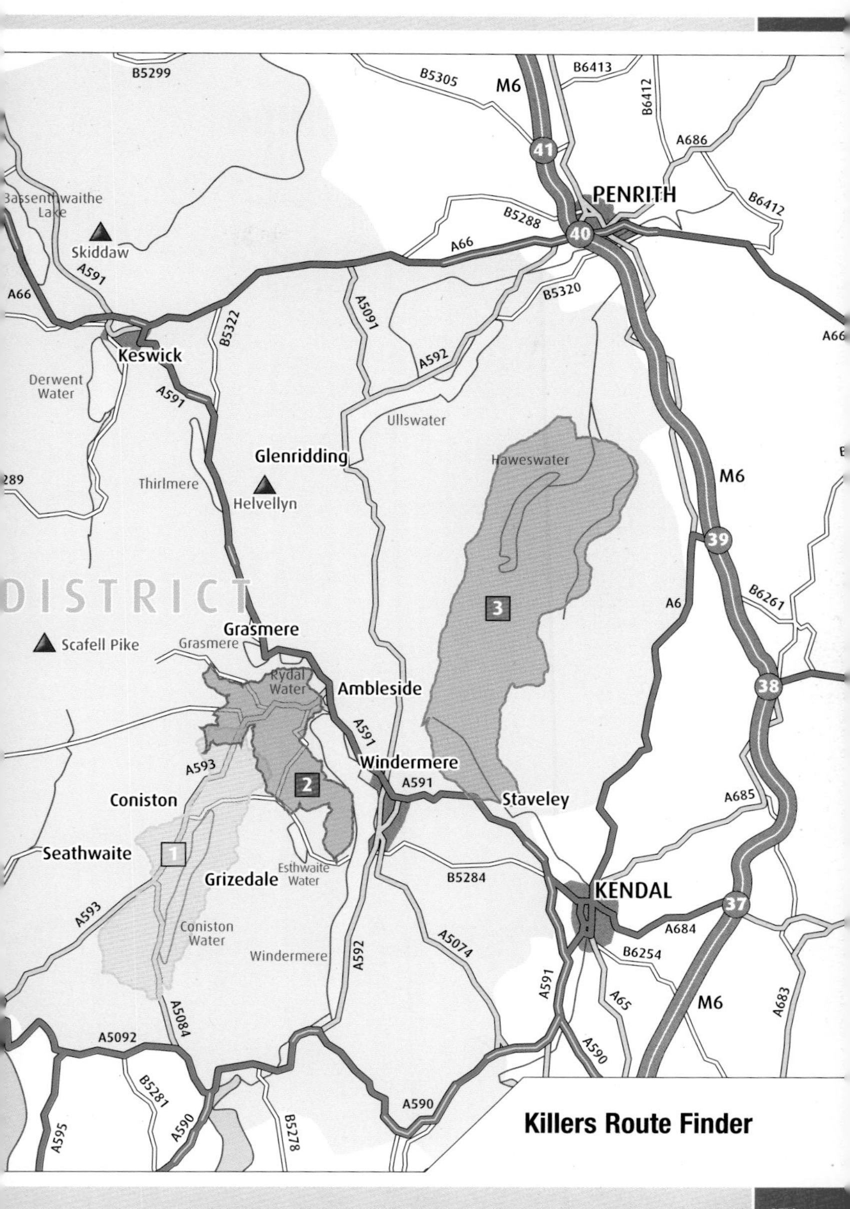
B5299
B5305
M6
B6413
B6412
A686
41
PENRITH
B6412
Bassenthwaithe Lake
Skiddaw
B5288
40
A66
A591
A66
B5320
A5091
B5322
A66
Keswick
A592
Derwent Water
A591
Ullswater
Glenridding
Haweswater
M6
Thirlmere
Helvellyn
39
DISTRICT
B6261
A6
3
Grasmere
Scafell Pike
Grasmere
Rydal Water
Ambleside
38
A591
Windermere
A593
2
A591
Coniston
Staveley
A685
Seathwaite
1
Esthwaite Water
Grizedale
B5284
KENDAL
37
A593
Coniston Water
A5074
A684
B6254
Windermere
A592
A591
A65
M6
A683
A5084
A5092
A590
B5281
A590
A595
A590
B5278
Killers Route Finder

Parkamoor & Tilberthwaite

40km

Introduction

A long(ish) ride circumnavigating Coniston Water. With the stunning views from Parkamoor, the remoteness of Blawith Fells, the exhilaration of descending Walna Scar road, the shock of civilisation in Coniston, the man-made landscape of Tilberthwaite quarries and the sheer beauty of Tarn Hows, this ride never has a dull moment!

The Ride

Starting from the forestry car park at High Cross, the route takes us south through Grizedale on great forest trails and then out over Parkamoor. Dropping down into the hamlet of High Nibthwaite on a classic south-Lakes descent, we continue south for a little while longer, before turning right to cross the River Crake. From here we climb away from Coniston on single-track over Blawith Fell and Woodland Fell. Reaching the A593, the route passes through the hamlet of Torver (two pubs here), and then leaves the road to start the climb up to Walna Scar. After a rocky descent into Coniston, we rejoin the A593 turning north heading for High Tilberthwaite. From here the route turns east to join the main Tarn Hows right of way which leads us back to Hawkshead Hill and finally High Cross.

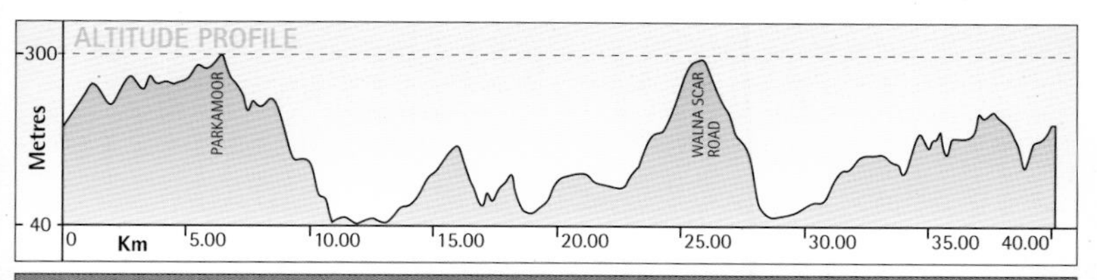

PARKAMOOR & TILBERTHWAITE — **GRADE: ▲**

DISTANCE: 40KM

TOTAL ASCENT: 1,284M

START/FINISH: HIGH CROSS

GRID REFERENCE: SD 332 986

PARKING: IN HIGH CROSS CAR PARK

CAFÉ: SEVERAL IN CONISTON

PUBLIC HOUSE: SEVERAL ALONG THE ROUTE

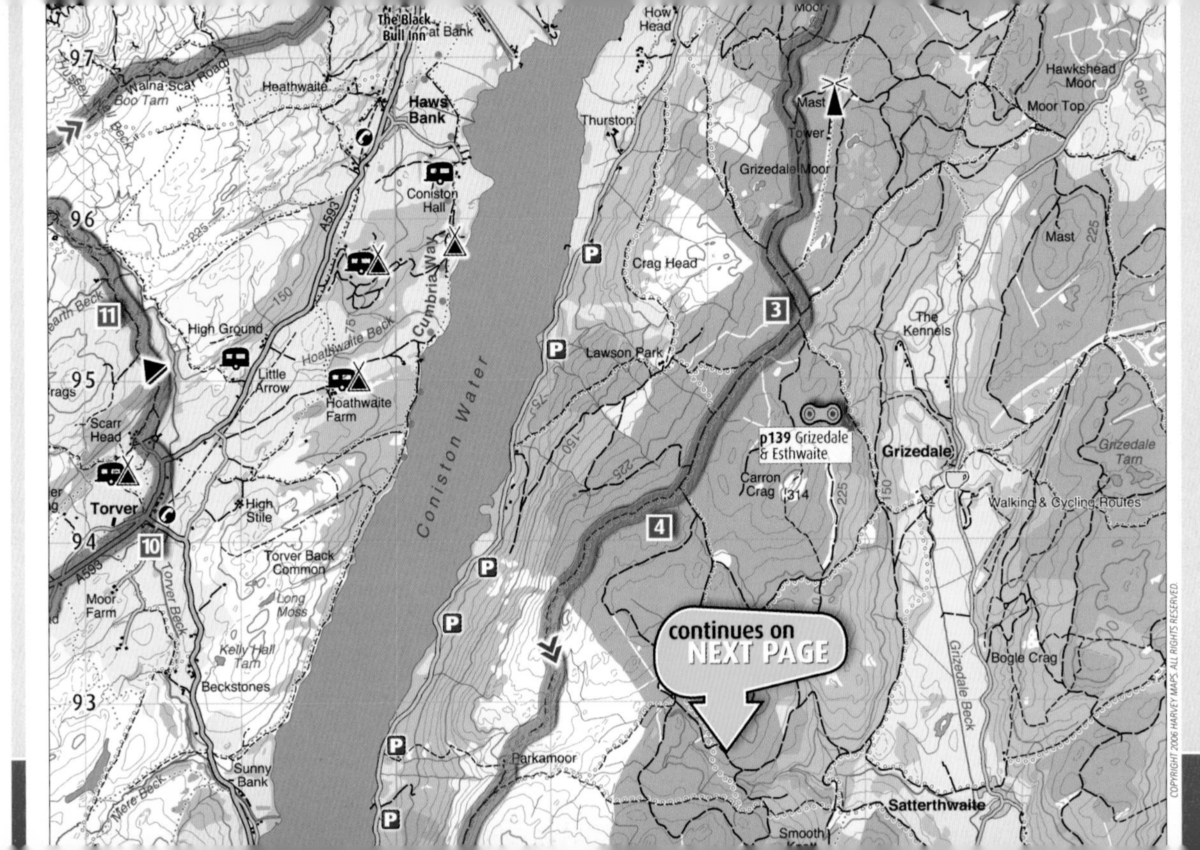

The Black Bull Inn at Bank
How Head
Hawkshead Moor
Moor Top
Walna Scar Road
Boo Tarn
Heathwaite
Haws Bank
Thurston
Mast
Tower
Grizedale Moor
Coniston Hall
Crag Head
Mast
Cumbria Way
A593
High Ground
Hoathwaite Beck
Little Arrow
Hoathwaite Farm
Lawson Park
The Kennels
Scarr Head
Torver
High Stile
Coniston Water
p139 Grizedale & Esthwaite
Carron Crag 314
Grizedale
Grizedale Tarn
Walking & Cycling Routes
Torver Back Common
Moor Farm
Torver Beck
Long Moss
Kelly Hall Tarn
Beckstones
continues on NEXT PAGE
Bogle Crag
Grizedale Beck
Sunny Bank
Mere Beck
Parkamoor
Satterthwaite
Smooth
97
96
95
94
93
11
10
3
4

Parkamoor & Tilberthwaite (Part 1)

continued from PREVIOUS PAGE
p7 Blawith Loop
p125 Grizedale & Parkamoor
Troughton Hall
Haverigg Holme
Steers Pool
The Knott
Woodland Grove
Hawes
Green Moor
Climb Stile
Spunham
Blawith Knott
Mere Sike
Coulter Stone
Yew Bank
Blawith Fells
Strands Beck
Beacon Tarn
Beacon Fell
Stable Harvey Moss
Coats Hill
Black Beck
Tottlebank
Cockenskell
Appletree Holme
Lin Crag Farm
Kiln Bank
Crooked Birch
Birch Bank
Ivy Tree
Blawith
Greenholme Beck
Lake Bank
High Nibthwaite
Water Yeat
Allan Tarn
Great Knott
Birk Row
Crake
Peel Island
Top o' Selside
Arnsbarrow Tarn
Tarn Beck
Caws Beck
High Bethecar
Stock
Hill Park Farm
Abbot Park
Bandrake Head
Oxen Park
Colton Beck
Satterthwaite Moor
A5084
A593

Parkamoor & Tilberthwaite (Part 2)

Directions – Parkamoor & Tilberthwaite 

S Leave High Cross car park on the forest road at the far end of the car park (away from the road), heading south into Grizedale. Continue **SA** on a narrower trail as the track bends left after a short climb. Follow this trail until it rejoins a forest road.

2 Turn **R** and continue **SA** for 1.5km across Monk Coniston Moor, passing a track on the right and climbing to a T-junction. Turn **R**, uphill, passing a second bridleway on the right as you descend to an offset crossroads. Turn **R** and then fork **R** almost immediately.

3 Continue along the forest track, passing a bridleway on the right, to a sharp left-hand bend. Continue **SA** between three large boulders onto singletrack marked with a bridleway sign to Parkamoor.

4 Follow this singletrack to the edge of the forest. Go through a gate onto an obvious trail out over Parkamoor, soon descending to a ruin. Pass in front of the ruin and descend between walls to a gate by a stream. Go through the gate in a ghostly type way and climb the hill ahead to a track. Turn **R** downhill (south) to start the superb South Lakes classic descent to High Nibthwaite.

5 Reaching High Nibthwaite in one piece, join the minor road and turn **L**. After 850m turn **R** onto a minor road opposite Arklid Farm. Cross the River Crake to join the A5084. Turn **L** onto the main road and continue south for another 850m to the village of Blawith.

6 Turn **R** up the minor lane opposite the church/phonebox/letterbox. Bear **R** at the fork and continue uphill. At the next fork after a cattle grid, bear **R** again. (The left branch is signed Tottlebank only.) After 800m the road reaches a T-junction. Turn **R** then immediately **L** onto a narrow bridleway signed *Woodland*.

7 Follow the obvious track, ignoring turnings, for some superb riding and climb to the highest point on Woodland Fell. At the summit, **ignore** a path to the left and keep to the bridleway. The descent doesn't fail to impress either but take care in your enthusiasm not to miss the **R** turn, marked by a small tree, after 900m.

8 The bridleway descends to cross a small river, and then climbs slightly to avoid a rather strangely positioned fence. Continue along this track, following the wall to a sharp left turn where the path climbs steeply, staying by the wall. At the top bear **R**, dropping to a small stream with a steep entry and exit (be sure to select the right gear). After fording the stream, the path bears **L** through a gap in the fence. Drop down before climbing to meet the main track. Turn **R** and climb along this before descending to Haverigg Holme.

9 At the foot of the descent, pass through two gates and join a metalled road. Follow this road for 2.75km to the A593. At the main road, turn **R** to Torver.

10 Follow the A593 through Torver (pub stop, if required) to a right-hand bend just outside the village. Turn **L** up a lane and climb the hill. Follow the lane, keeping **L** at the forks, climbing up around the **RH** hairpin and onto a signposted bridleway. The lane soon becomes a track with some quite challenging rocky steps and steep sections, but all good fun! Eventually the bridleway passes through a sheepfold and crosses a stream via a bridge. The path then starts to climb through an old slate quarry.

11 At the top of this lung-busting ascent, (more due to loose slate than to its length or steepness), the path becomes more forgiving. A fence appears on the left, preventing you from falling head first into a now-flooded disused quarry. Round this fence and continue the ascent. After a rather difficult rock step there is a choice of route. It's not crucial which path you choose, as they all lead to the main Walna Scar Road, but the preferred way is to bear **R**, drop down to the stream and climb the steep grassy bank in front of you and off to the right.

12 Upon reaching Walna Scar Road (the big wide track), regardless of your choice of route, turn **R**, descend to join tarmac and continue down into Coniston and a well-earned café stop (if you stopped in Torver as well then you're just being greedy). Drop into Coniston until you hit the main A593 Ambleside road. Turn **L** towards Ambleside.

13 Following the A593 go over the bridge in Coniston turn **L** by the Black Bull pub. Where the road becomes unmade, turn **R** onto the permitted bridleway. Follow this until it finishes on the A593, and turn **L** immediately onto the road signposted *Tilberthwaite* Follow this road to its end at High Tilberthwaite Farm. **Please dismount** and walk through the farmyard, taking the gate on the **R** once in the yard itself.

DIRECTIONS CONTINUE OVERLEAF

Parkamoor & Tilberthwaite – continued

14 Follow the well-made track, keeping **R** at the fork, for 1km and descend sharply to a T-junction. Turn **R** and descend, cross a stream and tackle the tricky climb. Turn **R** onto the main track at the top and climb to a metalled lane at some buildings.

15 Turn **L**, climbing around an S-bend and turn **R** right up the track to a gate. Continue **SA** along the track to its end at High Oxen Fell (farm). Go through the farm on to the metalled lane, bearing **R** at the junction and dropping down to the A593.

16 Cross the road with care and climb **SA** up the lane opposite, taking the **R** fork after a few metres on to a rough track. This is the main Tarn Hows/Arnside Intake right of way, so expect to meet motorised vehicles! Follow it for over 3km (tricky climbing and a fast descent) to its end at Knipe Fold. At the T-junction with the road, turn **R**. Climb up Hawkshead Hill, **ignoring** turnings to the left and right and, after 1.5km, continue **SA** over the main road into the car park at High Cross.

Making a day of it

You could tack the **Blawith Loop** *(page 07)* onto the southern end of this ride, explore **Walna Scar** *(page 161)* in to the west or play in the forest on the eastern side of the route.

TOM FENTON ON THE SINGLETRACK

MAKING A SPLASH ON THE BIG DAY OUT

Big Day Out

50km

Introduction

What a day out! This route is one of the best rides in the Lakes, taking in many of the best bridleways – some easy, some technical – making it a hard day. Covering a large number of the bridleways in the south-east Lakes (with the exception of Grizedale), the ride also requires a good deal of commitment, not to mention a considerable level of fitness. The route is generally low-lying, so can be undertaken at any time of the year, given reasonable conditions – the only point you might need to consider is the available daylight in winter.

The Ride

Starting by Brathay, just past Clappersgate, the ride heads south to Claife, along the shore of Windermere on easy tracks and around Claife, before heading east to Hawkshead. From there, rocky tracks lead over to Hodge Close and Tilberthwaite via Iron Keld. More rocky riding goes north towards Elterwater and then into Langdale, before the final run takes the great trails around Loughrigg, finally finishing in Ambleside.

Note: This is not a detailed description, as most of the route is a combination of other routes covered within this guide. Anyway, we have to leave some of it to a sense of adventure and your map reading skills!

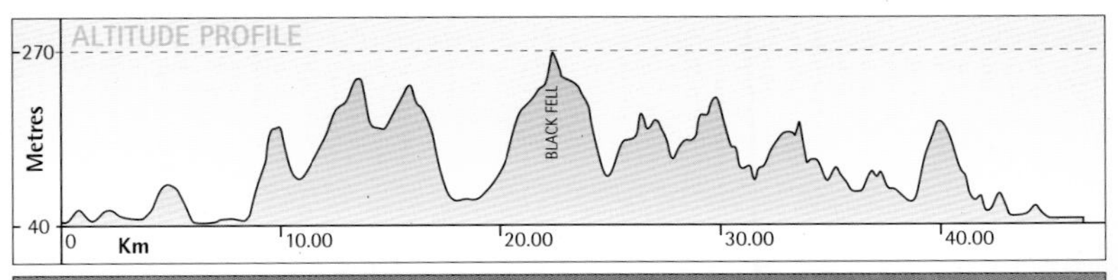

BIG DAY OUT **GRADE: ▲**

DISTANCE: 50KM

START/FINISH: BRATHAY

PARKING: BRATHAY (BY THE RIVER)

PUBLIC HOUSE: AMBLESIDE

TOTAL ASCENT: 1,500M

GRID REFERENCE: NY 366 034

CAFÉ: AMBLESIDE

NY
31
32
33
34
B5343
Langdale
Great Langdale Beck
Lang Howe
Silver Howe
Town End
White Moss
The Lea
Grasmere
Dale End
Langdale Boulders
Copt Howe
Thrang Crag
Raven Crag
Red Bank
Loughrigg Terrace
Oakhowe Crag
Lingmoor Tarn
Hag Wood
Chapel Stile
6
Upper Spout Crag
Bayes Brown
Britannia
Elterwater
Low Wood
Intake Wood
Oaks
Brown How
Lingmoor Fell
Sawrey's Wood
Banks Quarry
Cumbria Way
Nab Island
Elter Water
Loughrigg Tarn
Busk Pike
Bield Crag
Fletcher's Wood
Hacket
Little Langdale
Little Langdale Tarn
Colwith Force
Skelwith Force
Skelwith Bridge
Park How
A593
River Brathay
High Park
Cathedral Quarry
Moss Rigg Quarry
Runestone Quarry
Great How
Park Fell
Hodge Close
High Oxen Fell
Quarries
Hodge Close Quarry
Parrock Quarry
5
Blake Rigg
High Tilberthwaite
Black Fell
Tilberthwaite Quarry
Holme Fell
Long Crag
Raven
Tom
Yew
Sunny
Drunk Duck
06
05
04
03
02
01
405
470
322
317
414
335

Big Day Out (Part 1)

Tilberthwaite Quarry
Holme Fell
Raven Crag
Long Crag
Tom Heights
Yew Tree Tarn
Tarn Hows
Sunny Brow
Field House
High Yewdale
Yewdale Fells
Knipe Fold
Cumbria Way
Tarn Hows Wood
Tarn Hows Hotel
Sandy Ground
Yewdale Crag
Thurs Gill
Mart Crag
Rigg Head
Hawkshead Hill
p37, 125 & 139
Grizedale Forest Routes
Far End
Yewdale Beck
Boon Crag
Monk Coniston
Guards Wood
Coniston
Monk Coniston Moor
Cat Bank
How Head
Haws Bank
Hawkshead Moor
Mast
Moor Top
Thurston
Tower
Grizedale Moor
Coniston Hall
Crag Head
The Kennels
Lawson Park
Coniston Water
Grizedale
Grizedale Tarn
Carron Crag
A593
B5285

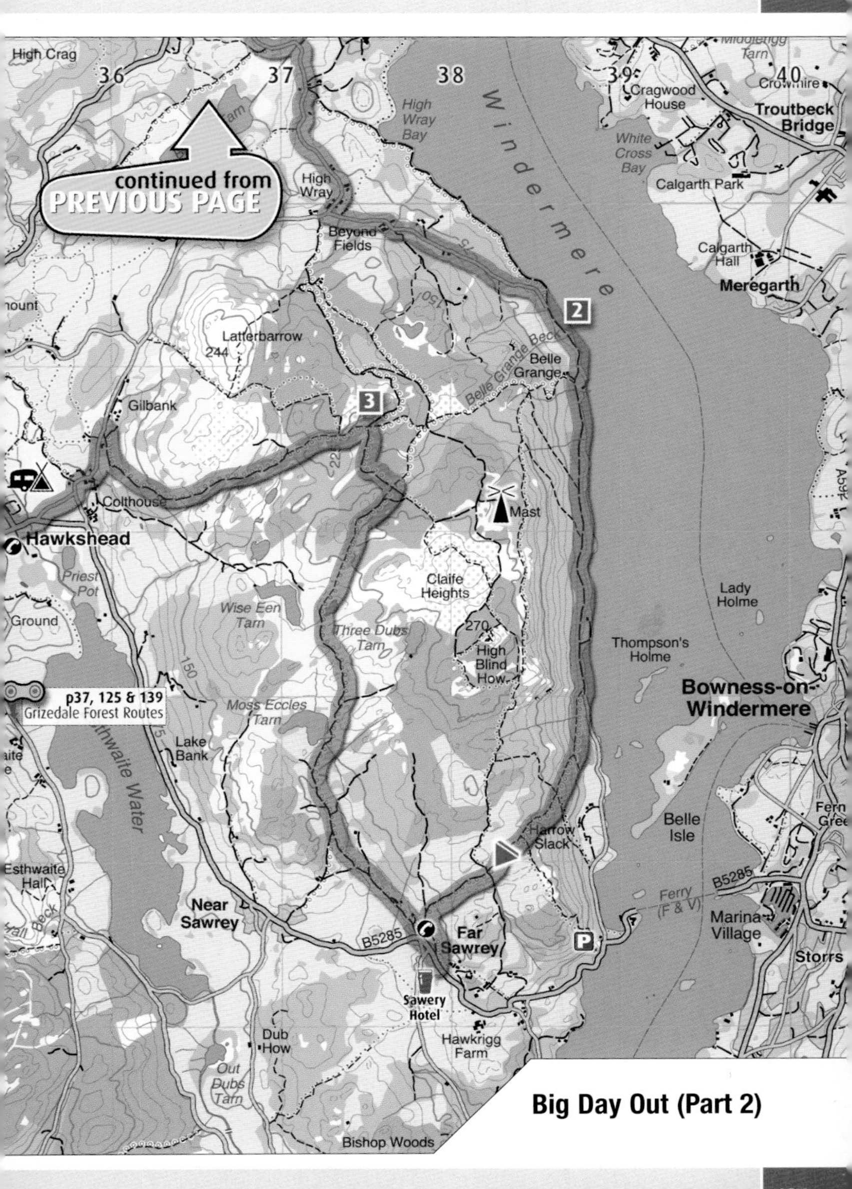
continued from
PREVIOUS PAGE
p37, 125 & 139
Grizedale Forest Routes
Windermere
Hawkshead
Colthouse
Latterbarrow
Gilbank
High Wray
Beyond Fields
Belle Grange
Claife Heights
Mast
Three Dubs Tarn
Wise Een Tarn
Moss Eccles Tarn
High Blind How
Lake Bank
Near Sawrey
Far Sawrey
Sawery Hotel
Hawkrigg Farm
Harrow Slack
Dub How
Out Dubs Tarn
Bishop Woods
Esthwaite Water
Esthwaite Hall
Priest Pot
Troutbeck Bridge
Cragwood House
Calgarth Park
Calgarth Hall
Meregarth
White Cross Bay
High Wray Bay
Lady Holme
Thompson's Holme
Bowness-on-Windermere
Belle Isle
Marina Village
Storrs
Ferry (F & V)
B5285
High Crag
Belle Grange Beck
Big Day Out (Part 2)

Directions – Big Day Out

S Head south along the B5286 (Hawkshead Road) and turn L towards Wray. At High Wray, turn L onto Claife Road (signed Ferry) and reverse the Claife Route (p 00 for more detailed directions).

2 Claife Road soon becomes a track. Follow this along the shoreline for just over 2km until you're opposite the Islands (Thompson Holme and Belle Isle), and turn R onto a bridleway that runs uphill. Follow this to Far Sawrey; turn R by the pub and then R again on a bridleway heading north.

3 At Guide Posts, leave the Claife Route and head east to Hawkshead. Once in Hawkshead, take the main road north-west signed Ambleside/Coniston, soon turning L for Coniston at Hall Bridge. Then take the next R onto Skinner Lane How, heading north-west to Knipe Fold.

4 The route has a bit of climbing now as it continues north-west through Knipe Fold and Iron Keld (reversing the Loughrigg and Elterwater route – p 00 – over the highest point on the ride). This brings you out on the A593. Turn L and head south to High Oxen. Turn R (onto Loughrigg & Elterwater route proper) here and head steeply uphill to Hodge Close, then north through Tilberthwaite.

5 Follow the wide stone track, climbing from Tilberthwaite and beginning to descend. Before arriving at Fell Foot Bridge, break off the Loughrigg route, turning R to Low Hall Garth and then to L to Little Langdale. Head to Elterwater via Dale End, turning L to Baysbrown Farm just after the gate on the descent to Elterwater. From here, continue along the bridleway to Oak Howe, cross Great Langdale Beck and turn R along the road, through Chapel Stile and towards Elterwater.

6 Just outside Elterwater, pick up the Loughrigg & Elterwater route once again and follow that route around Loughrigg Terrace to the Under Loughrigg road. Follow this back to Ambleside and back to the start. Enjoy!

Making a day of it

There's nothing stopping you dropping down into Grizedale for a quick loop of one of the rides there. Either nip south from Hawkshead, or head west from Far Sawrey to follow some of the forest trails up to rejoin the ride near Knipe Fold.

CLAIR LLOYD BESIDE WINDERMERE

STONE LANES IN KENTMERE

High Street & Swindale

60km

Introduction

High Street is one of the most spectacular and enjoyable rides in the Lake District. There are many ways of tackling it and this is probably one of the most arduous. The route follows the stunning ridge, taking the course of the old Roman road over High Street, High Raise and Wether Hill, then off towards Bampton Grange. The isolation of Swindale and Mosedale is breathtaking and is an area of the Lakes not often visited. It would be unusual to meet anyone here. This is a tough ride over high mountain terrain. Although not technically demanding, riders undertaking this route should be used to a long day. For the sake of route finding and enjoying the fantastic views, pick a clear day. You will need map-reading skills.

The Ride

This ride starts in Ings as it has a fine pub with a choice of ales (for when you get back). Getting to High Street always involves a climb and this route takes you up Park Fell with (more than) a bit of a push before following the old Roman road to Wether Hill. Vague trails lead to The Pen and farm lanes to Bampton Grange. Country lanes take you down the beautiful Swindale Valley until the valley rears up and you find yourself pushing again. Vague trails lead to Mosedale Cottage, (owned by the Mountain Bothy Association, and where you can spend the night if you wish). The trail becomes vague until you reach a gate, when it becomes non-existent. Join the Gatesgarth Pass, head to Sadgill and continue to Kentmere and a choice of finishes – Garburn Pass being one of them!

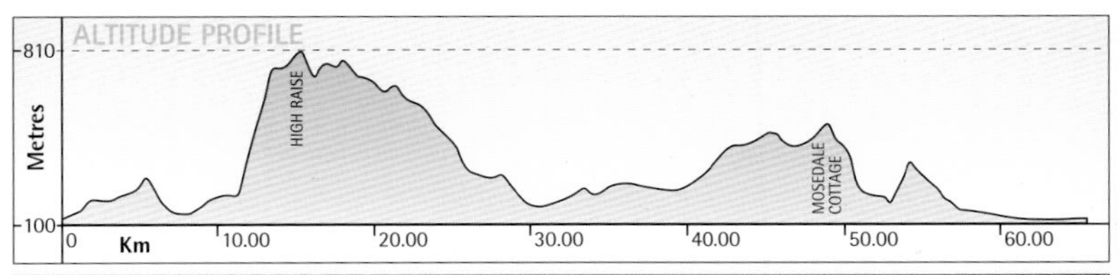

HIGH STREET & SWINDALE — **GRADE: ▲▲**

DISTANCE: 60KM

START/FINISH: WATERMILL INN, INGS

PARKING: SMALL CAR PARK AT INGS

PUBLIC HOUSE: WATERMILL INN, INGS Tel: 01539 821 309

TOTAL ASCENT: 1,932M

GRID REFERENCE: SD 444 987

CAFÉ: WILF'S, STAVELEY Tel: 01539 822 329

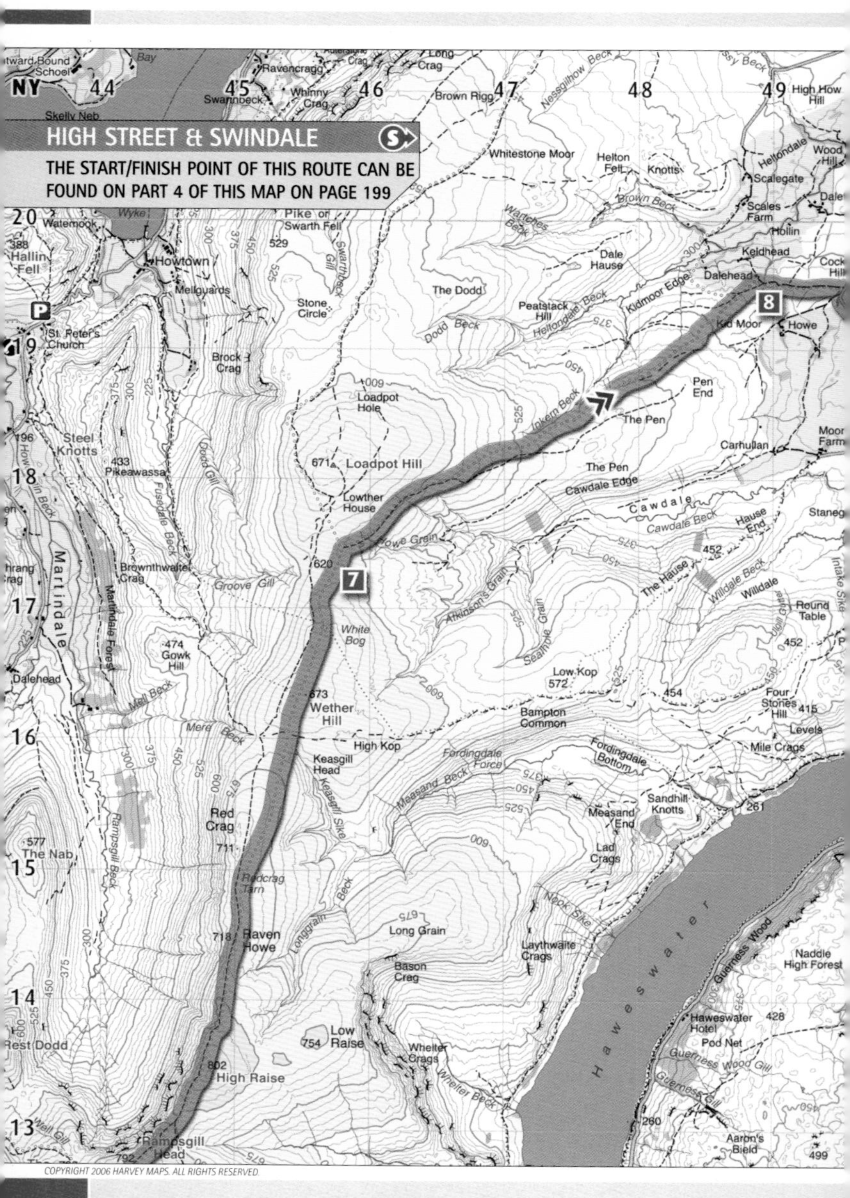
HIGH STREET & SWINDALE
THE START/FINISH POINT OF THIS ROUTE CAN BE FOUND ON PART 4 OF THIS MAP ON PAGE 199
Loadpot Hill
Wether Hill
High Raise
Low Raise
Haweswater
Howtown
Martindale
Bampton Common
Cawdale
Red Crag
Raven Howe
Kidmoor Edge
Haweswater Hotel
Gowk Hill
Steel Knotts
Pikeawassa
Brock Crag
The Dodd
Whitestone Moor
Helton Fell
Dale Hause
Scales Farm
Keldhead
Dalehead
Carhullan
Moor Farm
Low Kop
High Kop
Measand End
Lad Crags
Laythwaite Crags
Bason Crag
Long Grain
Whelter Crags
Rampsgill Head
Rest Dodd
The Nab

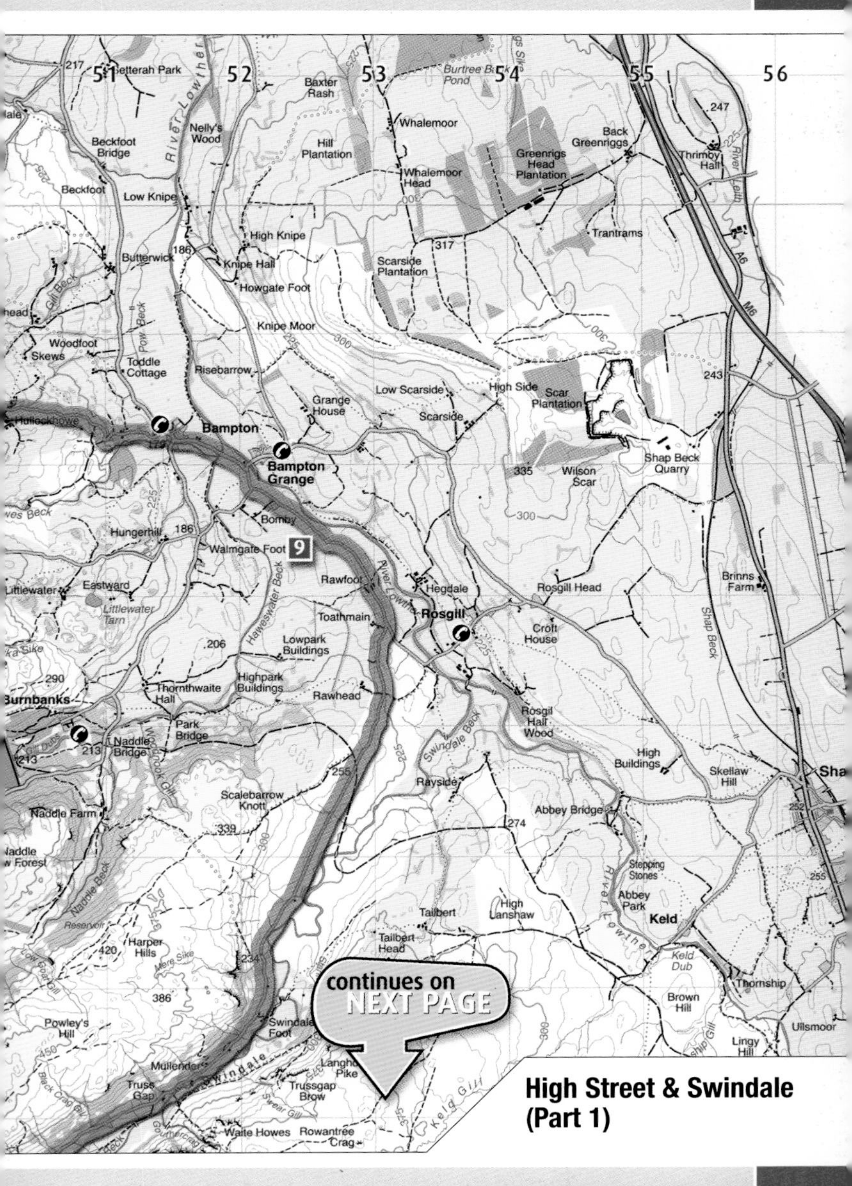

continues on NEXT PAGE

High Street & Swindale (Part 1)

NY
44
45
46
47
48
49
14
13
12
11
10
09
08
07
The Nab
Raven Howe
Long Grain
Lad Crags
Nook Sike
Laythwaite Crags
Haweswater
Guerness Wood
Naddle High Forest
Haweswater Hotel
Pod Net
Bason Crag
Low Raise
High Raise
Rest Dodd
Whelter Crags
Whelter Beck
Rampsgill Head
The Knott
Kidsty Pike
Twopenny Crag
Riggindale Straits
Short Stile
Kidsty Howes
Birks Crag
Flakehow Crag
Whiteacre Crag
Brownhowe Crags
Mardale Banks
Aaron's Bield
Speaking Crag
Wood Howe
Brown Howe
Old Corpse Road
High Loup
Low Loup
Hollow Stone
Mardale Common
Riggindale Beck
Riggindale Crag
Long Stile
Caspel Gate
Rough Crag
Eagle Crag
Heron Crag
Swine Crag
The Rigg
Hide
Boat Howe
Selside Pike
High Street
Blea Water Crag
Blea Water
Mardale Head
Brant Street
Swirle Crag
Artlecrag Pike
Survey Post
Branstree
Mardale Ill Bell
Plot Crag
Small Water
Small Water Crags
Harter Crag
Bleathwaite Crag
Gavel Crag
Hall Cove
Lingmell End
Nan Bield Pass
Harter Fell
Little Harter Fell
Gatescarth Pass
Gatescarth Beck
Selside Brow
Adam Seat
Mosedale Quarry (dis)
Mosedale Cottage
The Knowe
Drygrove Gill
Over Cove
Froswick
Kentmere Reservoir
Wrengill Quarry (dis)
Brownhowe Bottom
Brown Howe
Steel Rigg
Steel Pike
Kentmere Pike
Ill Bell
The Tongue
Raven Crag
Tarn Crag
Buckbarrow Crag
Rainsborrow Cove
Star Crag
Tongue Scar
Tongue House
Rainsborrow Crag
Goat Scar
Quarry Brow
River Kent
River Sprint
6
5
12

High Street & Swindale (Part 2)

Directions – High Street & Swindale

S From Ings, cross the road via the cycle path. Where the cycle path ends, turn **R** onto Moorhouse Road, signed *Heaning, Mislet*.

2 Continue along this road for 3km. Look out for a sign to High Borrans on the right. Shortly after this sign, turn **R** onto a wide bridleway to Dubbs Reservoir as the road bears left. Follow this good bridleway for 2.5km, passing Dubbs Reservoir and turn **L** back on yourself (straight ahead through the gate is the Garburn Pass) for a fun downhill.

3 After 500m turn sharp **R** and head north along the valley until the river can be crossed, via a footbridge by an old building, to another track. Turn **R** and head north on this, don't look too far ahead: you may not want to see where you're going!

4 As you approach Park Fell, the gradient starts to rear up quite considerably and by the time you go through a gate in a wall (continue **SA**) you will probably be pushing your bike (there is about half an hour of very steep terrain). As the wall curves away to the left, bear **R** on the bridleway, climbing steeply.

DIRECTIONS CONTINUE OVERLEAF

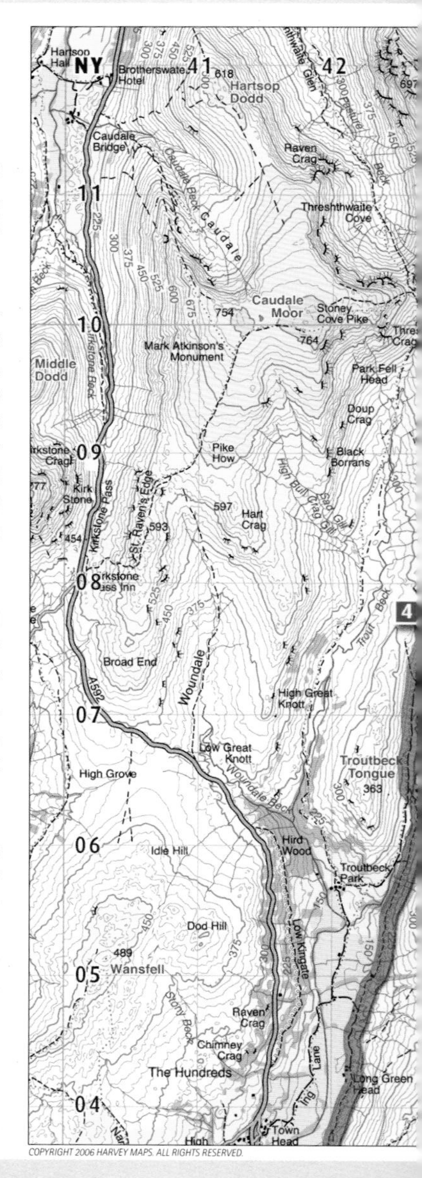

Riggindale Straits
44
45
46
47
48
49
Kidsty Howes
Speaking Crag
Wood Howe
Brown Howe
Old Corpse Road
Short Stile
Hide
Riggindale Beck
Low Loup
Hollow Stone
Mardale Common
Riggindale Crag
Eagle Crag
Heron Crag
Swine Crag
The Rigg
Long Stile
Caspel Gate
Rough Crag
Boat Howe
Selside Pike
Selside 655
828
High Street
Blea Water Crag
Blea Water
482
Brant Street
Hopegill Beck
Swirle Crag
618
Captain Whelter Bog
Mardale Head
Blea Water Beck
Small Water Beck
Woodfell Gill
Mardale Ill Bell
761
Plot Crag
Small Water
Harter Crag
Bleathwaite Crag
Small Water Crags
Gavel Crag
Hall Cove
Nan Bield Pass
629
Gatesgarth Beck
continued from
PREVIOUS PAGE
Mosedale Quarry (dis)
Mosedale Cottage
Great Grain Gill
Lingmell End
778
Harter Fell
Little Harter Fell
582
Gatescarth Pass
Selside Brow
Adam Seat 666
Wren Gill
Over Cove
River Kent
The Knowe
Brownhowe Bottom
Seavy Side
Froswick 720
Lingmell Gill
Drygrove Gill
Wrengill Quarry (dis)
423
Kentmere Reservoir
Brown Howe
Steel Rigg
Steel Pike
Ill Bell
757
Kentmere Pike
730
664
Tarn Crag
595
Raven Crag
Buckbarrow Crag
Greycrag Tarn
Grey Crag
298
The Tongue
Ullstone Gill
Rainsborrow Cove
Star Crag
Tongue Scar
River Sprint
Tongue House
Rainsborrow Crag
627
Goat Scar
706
Yoke
Galeforth Brow
Galeforth Gill
Longsleddale
Skeel Crags
Great Howe
Shipman Knotts 587
Skeel Gill
Bryant's Gill
Hartrigg
Withered Howe
Brock Crag
Overend
Sadgill
Saletarn Knotts
Sadgill Wood
continues on
NEXT PAGE
Hallow Bank
Brockstones
Whirl Howe
Stockdale
Buck Crag
Wray Crag
Castle Crag
Hill's Hole
Stockdale Bridge
Piked Hows
173
Tom's Howe
High Barn
Ewe Crags
Force Jump
Swinklebank Wood
Cocklaw Fell
Badger Rock
Nunnery Beck
449 Garburn Pass
Hall Gill
516
Sallows or Kentmere Park
Kentmere
Green Quarter
426
Kill Gill
High Street & Swindale (Part 3)

5 The bridleway eventually relents. Keep going north north-east to join the main track from Frostwick. Turn **L**. At the two metal fence posts, bear **R** on the bridleways as the ground falls steeply away to the right (**ignore** the well-trodden footpath that bears towards Thornthwaite Beacon). Continue **SA** until, after a short distance, the bridleway splits again. Take the **LH** fork.

6 The main bridleway takes you to below the summit of High Street on good, obvious tracks, and then heads downhill north to a junction of two bridleways. Turn **R** (north east). You get a stunning view of Hayeswater at this point. Follow good tracks along the ridge, leading north to High Raise, Red Crag and Wether Hill.

7 As you descend from Wether Hill you will probably be on a track to the left of the main bridleway. You need to fork **R** at **GR NY 458 174** on a bridleway before beginning to climb. The bridleway is, unfortunately, not easily visible on the ground. If you start going uphill and arrive at a cairn that is part of the old ruin (marked *Lowther House* on the map) you have gone too far. Follow the bridleway to contour around the hill without loosing too much height. Eventually you will be able to see two vague trails ahead on The Pen.

DIRECTIONS CONTINUE OVERLEAF

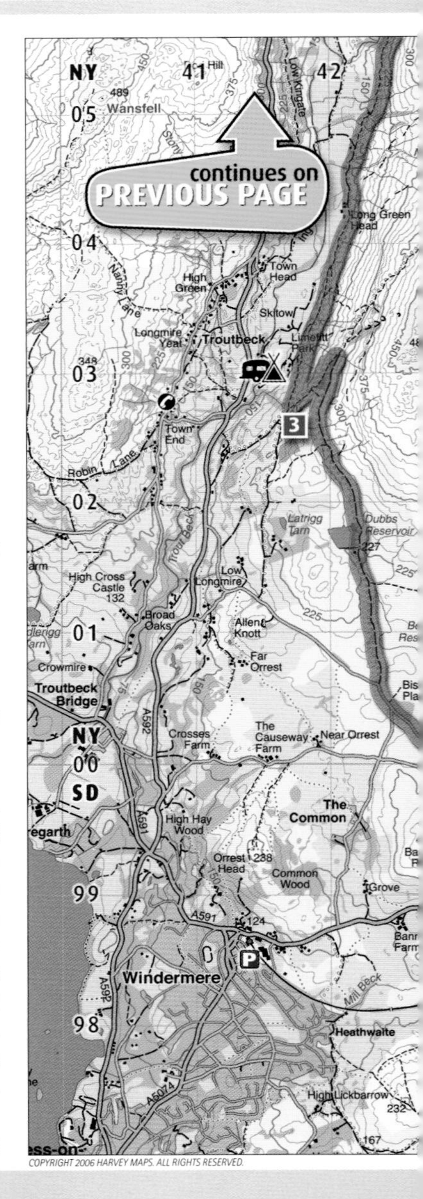

High Street & Swindale (Part 4)

Take the **LH** trail for a great downhill. You should pass a cairn to your right in the middle of a field, do not go to this, it seems to be there for no reason. (If it is on your left you are on the wrong track.)

8 At the good farm track by Dalehead, turn **R** and **R** again at the road. Go over a cattle grid and through a gate at Rough Hill Farm. Bear **R** through the buildings to another gate and continue on a gated road to a T-junction. Turn **L** and follow the road to Bampton (village store, pub and café). Turn **R** at the T-junction and keep left at the next to Bampton Grange. Just before the sharp left turn over the bridge, turn **R**, bearing **L** at the next junction, signed *Swindale*.

9 Continue along this lane for just over 1km and turn **R**, signed *Swindale 3 miles*. This lane takes you to the idyllic spot of Swindale. Continue **SA** at a crossroads onto a gated road for 4km to Swindale Head. As the road ends, continue riding **SA** for a short distance until it is no longer possible; a short(ish) push then brings you to the top of Nabbs Crag. The trail now becomes vague, so contour round to **L** of the craggy knoll and then bear back **R** to a fence with a gate at the right-hand side.

10 Once through the gate, the bridleway is a little better defined and follows the line of an old wall. **Ignore** the obvious trail, which takes you to a footbridge (although if you do find yourself here, do not cross the bridge but bear back **R**, to rejoin the main trail). From here the trail leads to Mosedale Cottage. This bothy is always open but **please clear up after yourself** if you use the facility (for further information **www.moutainbothies.org.uk**).

11 The trail from here is tough going due to the nature of the terrain and can be boggy after wet weather. Head towards a gated fence on vague trails. Beyond the gate, the trail becomes non-existent. Take a compass bearing of **252°** and head downhill – carefully, as you will have to change course and wind your way through this boggy and craggy terrain.

12 Finally you reach the more obvious Gatesgarth Pass at the bottom of the valley. Did you find the bridleway sign? Were you above it, below it or on it? Turn **L** and head downhill fast, this terrain is hard on your arms, not technical, but a long descent, with lots of vibration.

13 At Sadgill, turn **R** over the bridge, turning left shortly afterwards at the bridleway sign and then **R** in front of the farm to a gate. The track climbs gradually in a southerly direction through Sadgill Woods and then on to another gate.

14 Beyond the gate, continue **SA** up the steep track. (**Ignore** the bridleway to the left.) This is a good technical downhill, but unfortunately you're going up it! The track eventually plateaus and a fun downhill ensues (with a few gates). You eventually join the road at High Lane. Turn **L** through a gate onto a fast downhill – **be careful** here as the bends are blind to cars.

Option 1. Turn **R** at the first road (goes back acutely) and descend to Low Bridge. Turn **R** to Kentmere Church. If you're not tired enough at this point, continue over the Garburn Pass *(see page 25 for directions)* and back to your car.

Option 2. However if you are a little fatigued, take the bridleway to the left of the church and descend to Kentmere Hall. Go through the gate and struggle uphill – on good trails so no getting off apart from at the gates! After Whiteside End, an undulating, mainly downhill trail leads to a gate in a wall. Bear **R** over the stream as the bridleway forks and follow the good trail over open fell and through gates until a gate with signposts. Turn **L**, signed *Grassgarth* for another exhilarating downhill. At the fork, bear **R**, eventually to Grassgarth and a metalled road. Follow this back to Ings. At the next junction carry on along the road and to Staveley. Turn **R** at Staveley and continue on the cycle path back to Ings.

Tourist Information Centres

Ambleside	T: 01539 432 582
Bowness	T: 01539 442 895
Coniston	T: 01539 441 533
Keswick	T: 01768 772 645

Bike shops

Keswick Mountain Bikes, Keswick
T: **01768 780 586**

Lakeland Pedlar, Keswick
T: **01768 775 752**

Wheelbase, Staveley
T: **01539 821 443**

Ghyllside Cycles, Ambleside
T: **01539 433 592**

Biketreks, Ambleside
T: **01539 431 245**

Grizedale Mountain Bikes, Grizedale
T: **01229 860 335**

Millennium Cycles, Staveley
T: **01539 821 167**

Gill Cycles, Ulverston
T: **01229 581 116**

Bike Hire

Keswick Mountain Bikes, Keswick
T: **017687 75202**

Wheelbase, Staveley
T: **01539 821 443**

Grizedale Mountain Bikes, Grizedale
T: **01229 860 369**

Windermere Canoe Kayak, Bowness
T: **01539 444 451**

Country Lanes, Windermere
T: **01539 444 544**

Weather

www.bbc.co.uk/weather OR **www.metoffice.com**

Food and Drink

Cafés

There are hundreds of cafés around, so we have only listed two of our favourites. As you are probably aware the majority of pubs also have good catering particularly in the Lake District. See the individual rides for more.

Wilf's, Staveley
T: **01539 822 329**

Bluebird Café, Coniston
T: **01539 441 649**

Pubs

Again, there are loads – there's pretty much one in every village. See the individual rides for our recommendations. Here is a list of a few:

Eagle & Child, Staveley
T: **01539 821 320**

Watermill Inn, Ings
T: **01539 821 309**

Golden Rule, Ambleside
T: **01539 433 363**

Woolpack Inn, Boot
T: **01946 723 230**

Gilpin Bridge Inn, Gilpin Bridge
T: **01539 552 206**

Masons Arms, Cartmel Fell
T: **01539 568 486**

Prince Of Wales, Foxfield, Broughton
T: **01229 716 238**

Red Lion, Lowick Bridge
T: **01229 885 366**

Eagles Head, Satterthwaite
T: **01229 860 237**

Newfield Inn, Seathwaite
T: **01229 716 208**

Accommodation

For **youth hostels** please visit **www.yha.org.uk**
There are hostels in the following places:

Keswick	T: 0870 770 5894
Derwent Water	T: 0870 770 5792
Helvellyn	T: 0870 770 5862
Patterdale	T: 0870 770 5986
Borrowdale	T: 0870 770 5706
Grasmere	T: 0870 770 5836
Langdale	T: 0870 770 5908
Coniston Coppermines	T: 0870 770 5772
Hawkshead	T: 0870 770 5856
Honister House	T: 0870 770 5870
Ambleside	T: 0870 770 5672
Elterwater	T: 0870 770 5816
Eskdale	T: 0870 770 5824
Kendal	T: 0870 770 5892

Hotels, Self-Catering and B&B

Your best bet is to contact the **Tourist Information Centre** nearest to where you plan to ride or search the internet.

Camping

There are campsites all over the Lake District. All you've got to do is get a map, look for camping symbols and find one you like. They vary tremendously depending on what you're looking for and are very easy to find, so we're not going to list any here.

Windermere Ferry

(For Claife and Grizedale)

Summer Weekday 06:50, every 20mins, until 21:25
Summer Sunday 06:50, every 20mins, until 21:25
Winter Weekday 06:50, every 20mins, until 20:50
Winter Sunday 09:50, every 20mins, until 20:50

Other Publications

Off Road Trails and Quiet Lanes – Cycling in the Lake District and Yorkshire Dales –
Keith Bradbury, Vertebrate Graphics

Where to Mountain Bike in Britain –
Nicky Crowther, Open Air Books

About the Authors

Chris Gore

Chris Gore is better known for his rock climbing escapades. It is little known that he has been riding bikes since his first tricycle, starting in London and finally seeing good sense and finishing in the Lakes (there are no mountains in London). Chris enjoys both road and MTB and throws himself down rocky slopes on a regular basis, hey it's faster than walking.

Richard Staton

I started mountain biking back in Bristol in 1991 on a *Trek 970* whilst on a student work placement from Sheffield City Polytechnic. Being based most of the time in Sheffield those early years were spent riding in The Peak District. After graduation I moved to the South Lakes where I stayed in order to feed my addiction. More than ten years on, I'm still here and still ridin'!

About the photographer

At the end of each Peak District ride, Andy regrets living at the top of a big, steep hill on the outskirts of Matlock. A professional sports photographer, his twenty years as a mountain biker have included trips to Ethiopia, Romania, Morocco and China, and racing wins in *Polaris, Trailquest* and the 1,097-mile *Iditasport Impossible* across Alaska. He can be contacted on **01629 580 780** or at **andrew.heading@btopenworld.com**

Vertebrate Graphics

Vertebrate Graphics (VG) is Britain's leading graphic design agency that specialises in the outdoor leisure market. Based deliberately near the Peak District, the guidebook production team spend as much time as they can walking, riding and climbing in the Peak District. We have had substantial success in the design and production of specialist outdoor books. These include *Hillwalking – The Official Handbook of the Mountain Leader and Walking Group Leader Schemes* (a bestselling outdoor title for three years running), the highly praised rock climbing guidebooks such as *The Roaches – Staffordshire Grit* and the UK's best selling mountain bike guide: *Dark Peak Mountain Biking – True Grit Trails.*

VG produce printed literature, advertising and websites, for more details of our services please refer to our website at: **www.v-graphics.co.uk** or email us at: **info@v-graphics.co.uk**

Notes

Notes

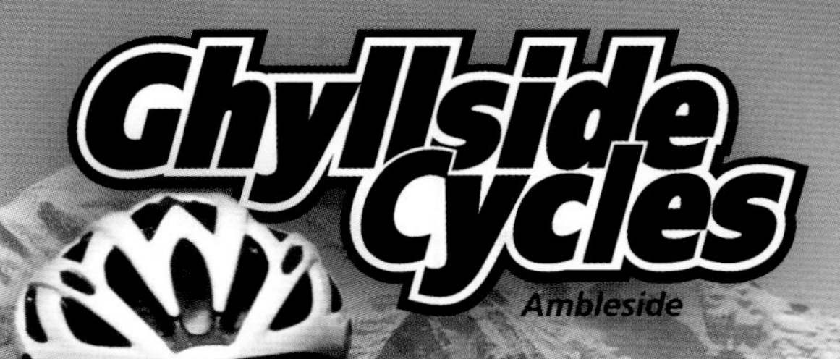
Ghyllside Cycles
Ambleside